Love's Body Speaks

Love's Body Speaks

by Caitlin Adair

Embodying the Sacred Feminine
in the New Millennium

Cover of the First Edition of Love's Body Speaks, 1996
Drawing by Dorothy Osterman
Calligraphy by Elizabeth Chapman

Copyright © 2018 by Caitlin Adair
All rights reserved.

Published by Sanctuary
40 Gregg Road
Westminster West, VT 05346
www.caitlinadair.com
www.sanctuaryvermont.com

Cover design: Julia Eva Bacon
Cover photo: Caitlin Adair
Author photo: Tony Bacon

ISBN 978-1-365-88220-3

Dedication

To All My Relations:
I love you and thank you for my life

♥

CONTENTS

Foreword		1
Introduction		3
Chapter 1:	**In the Beginning**	5
	Stories	
	About the Universe Story and Love	
	And God said CREATE	
	Addiction to Things	
Chapter 2:	**Sonata to Eros** in 5 Movements	15
Chapter 3:	**Development of a Species**	25
	Journey of a Species	
	Prehistoric and Historic Archetypal Male/Female Relations by Peter Adair	
Chapter 4:	**Through a Doorway**	45
	Moon Magic and Hunt Magic	
	Sacrifice; Blood Mysteries	
	Art as Doorway to Sacred Consciousness	
Chapter 5:	**Under Her Skirts**	73
	The Deep She – Parts 1 and 2	
	The Core and The Well	
Chapter 6:	**Sacred Sex**	81
	Wall of Lies	
	About Peter and Me	
	Symbolism of Male and Female Genitalia	
	Making Love	
	Pleasure-bonding and Erotiphobia	
	The Original Blueprint	

| Chapter 7: | **Women, Religion and Lies** | 105 |

Why women have trouble with Patriarchal religions; Religions of the Book;

Spiritual Sexual Abuse;

In love with the Father God

Vomiting Woman

Why we are destroying our ecosystems

| Chapter 8: | **Goddess** | 129 |

Goddess is a verb

FAX to Bethlehem

How the most sacred turned into the most profane

| Chapter 9: | **Emotions** | 135 |

The war between Mind and Body

Most Valuable Advice

Authentic Movement

Body Logic; Mind Games

Bliss & Awe; Ecstasy and Religion

ALIVE!; The Big Picture

| Chapter 10: | **Moving Toward Wholeness** | 157 |

The Stacked Deck; How to Change

Art Births the Artist; Enactment

The Bottom Line

| The Last Chapter | 167 |

References and Recommended Reading	171
Acknowledgements	173
About the Author	174

viii

Foreword

Caitlin has offered the courageous and authentic voice of a wise woman in *Love's Body Speaks*. Her lived experience and the life transitions and transformations she weathered on her way to that wisdom will resonate with many women. Her exploration of the interconnected flow of life and growth in our species gives us hope for a new day...beyond gender, duality and divisiveness. *Love's Body Speaks* is a call to humanity to mature into an adult species that cares for its members and its home.

Along the way, Caitlin calls for women to embody their physical/emotional nature and embrace their creative power, sexuality, and inner knowing. She sheds light on the history that got us where we are today, while helping us to shed the old wineskin, making way for an evolved and elevated womankind.

Men too, will find validation and guidance in *Love's Body Speaks* as Caitlin encourages them to integrate the feminine qualities that will make men whole. This is something our planet and the future of the species needs now more than ever, an enlightened leadership that will protect, preserve and serve humanity.

I encourage you to take this journey with Caitlin, through the past, present and future. Using story, art, music, dance and theatre, we can release and reveal the inner knowing of a shared planetary and cosmic adventure while healing from our collective past. Step out and in to find the yin to your yang. The dance is sweet and the air is clear....come along!

Reverend Mary Francis Drake, LICSW

Introduction to the Second Edition

Love's Body Speaks is largely the result of the work that my partner Peter Adair and I did together from the time of our meeting in 1987 until 1996, exploring the intersection of sexuality and spirituality in our relationship and in the context of what it has meant to be a human being throughout the history of the species.

Our insights are presented in the form of embodied teachings, combining history, personal narrative and bodily experience in order to give the most complete picture as we understood it. I invite you to consider that these writings have come to a particular woman with a particular life experience who, like the rest of us, cannot separate her emotions from her opinions and feels that to do so would be a betrayal of the wholeness of self. Although I cannot speak for every woman, my desire is to feel into the experience of Womankind in relation to the whole, and to report it here to you.

In creating this second edition, I have omitted certain sections from the first edition and have made a few updates, but am happy to see that the work still stands strongly in its truth.

C. A., Feb. 22, 2018

Chapter 1

In the Beginning

Dream of the Wise Woman:

> *It is a sunny winter's day with a dusting of snow. Peter and I go to visit a friend who lives on beautiful land owned by several members of his family who also live there. We walk through a large field with red brick paths crossing it. Beautiful trees surround the field and buildings, which are not new but are beautifully kept and well loved. The whole place is FULL OF PRESENCE. We go into the house, which is small and cozy. An older woman is there, the wise woman of the family. She has something important to tell me, wants me to write it down. I write inside the cover of a book. I am listening very carefully. She gives me a tiny pin portraying the head and hands of a baby who is emerging as though from a pocket. It is so tiny. Awkwardly I try to figure out how to wear it.*

Stories

"Human beings live by stories. Whatever the story is that you tell yourself consciously or unconsciously, that is the life you will bring forth. Choose your stories carefully. The old storytellers of Native America tell us *"Beloved, the real power of the story is that as you tell it, it begins to happen."* "

~Elizabeth Cogburn

"What is the human? The human is a space, an opening, where the universe celebrates its existence."

~Brian Swimme

O Mother

Guide me.

Guide my hand as I write your/our story.

Guide my intelligence, that which allows me to pull together disparate threads of meaning.

The love of the story, the love unfolding from seed to sapling to tree, its flowerings fertilized by bees, the small fruit forming, swelling, ripening, coloring, sweetening.

The love of the growing, the telling, the movement.

As far as we know, humans are the only species able to perceive and express the stories of existence from the smallest to the largest, from atom to elephant to galaxy. We are the self-reflecting organ of the Universe. By perceiving, exploring, dreaming and reflecting upon an ever-expanding reality, we have come to know ourselves and our world.

With our intricate gifts of communicating with language, gesture, art and music, we gather around the campfire or the TV to hear stories both spoken and sung. We read books to learn the stories, fiction and nonfiction. We explore space and the minutiae of our Earth to learn the stories, but in science we call them 'facts.' Facts connected are stories just the same. Songs are stories. Paintings are stories, buildings are stories, machines are stories. What is all this curiosity except a driving desire to learn the stories of everything we see-hear-taste-touch, and then with joy fashion new creations with stories of their own?

Being in the story

Where else to be?
You're either in the story or you're nowhere.
Untouchable: the death curse
is to be no longer in the story of your people.
Who are your people?
Do we need a people to have a story?
What are people for?
> -to be in it
> -to watch it
> -to create it.

Be in it.
Be with
> the myth.

About the Universe Story and Love

> "We are discovering anew our capacity for entering into the larger community of life...There is eventually only one story, the story of the universe. Every form of being is integral with this comprehensive story. **Nothing is itself without everything else.** Each member of the Earth community has its own proper role within the entire sequence of transformations that have given shape and identity to everything that exists...Without entrancement within this new context of existence it is unlikely that the human community will have the psychic energy needed for the renewal of the Earth."
>
> ~*Thomas Berry and Brian Swimme*

The Universe Story

This story is about how we really are connected to all things. Science has proven it, and if you would like to learn some of the exhilarating details, I recommend reading The Universe Story by Brian Swimme and Thomas Berry. My husband found a new reason for living when he discovered The Universe Story, because it unites his three loves: science, mysticism and mythology. The Universe Story places us in time and space, smack in the middle of the amazing true tale of the birth, evolution and death (stay tuned) of THE UNIVERSE. It gives us white folks what we have not had since Copernicus: a cosmology that is up to date with the scientific knowledge of our time.

The Universe Story ties together the smallest particles with the largest, seeing patterns, shapes and movements of electrons mirrored in galaxies. The Universe Story is awe-inspiring in scope and in its likely ultimate effect upon human consciousness, for when knowledge of this grandest of stories seeps into the general awareness, humans will realize that nothing is random, that they themselves and every part of their experience are part of a radiant intelligent being striving to know itself in a beautiful blossoming that began with the Cosmic Birth and continues into this very moment.

Doorway

While living in England in 1986, I attended a seminar on transformation of consciousness with Dr. Richard Moss titled "The I That Is We." A profound turning point for me, the seminar provided many breakthroughs leading to a significant shedding and shredding of my concepts of reality. One particularly powerful exercise was called the Cross of Gold. We paired off facing each other, put our arms out to the side as if on a cross, and with our eyes locked, sang over and over *"How I Love You"* to a booming recording of the stately Pachelbel Canon. FOR ONE HOUR we stood and sang, without lowering our arms. The pain in my shoulders seemed unbearable, but the miracle expressed and received in the voice and eyes of a stranger gave me strength I did not know I possessed. "How I love you!" meant "I see you, I love you, I am Here for you." It went in deep.

Image the human: soulspirit
Mystical marriage of sun to earth, energy to matter
United by the spark of love recognized in the eye
Of the other who is no longer other

The revelation on the Cross of Gold was this: the love of Spirit and Matter is the motivating force in the Universe. Standing crucified, I became Matter (mater, mother, maya, fertile ground, dark mystery). Facing me was Spirit taking the form of a strong, beautiful male (spiritus, breath, light, father, sower of seed). *"How I Love You"* we sang to each other's soul.

My experience of the love of Spirit and Matter became a cornerstone for my new house-of-self. I offer it as a metaphysical, alchemical truth: the motivating force behind all movement, be it molecular or galactic, is the love of the male principle for the female principle and the female for the male. Not love as emotion, but as the deep abiding irresistible desire of opposites to come together, creating something new. Mark these words: *it is love that animates everything.*

> *"Now you can understand what love means: love is a word that points to alluring activity in the cosmos. This primal dynamism awakens the communities of atoms, galaxies, stars, families, nations, persons, ecosystems, oceans, and stellar systems. Love ignites being."*
>
> ~Brian Swimme, cosmologist

> *"To dismiss love as the biological basis of social life, and also the ethical implications of love, would be to turn our back on a history as living beings that is more than 3.5 billion years old...Love is a biological dynamic with deep roots."*
>
> ~Humberto Maturana, biologist, and
> Francisco Varela, neuroscientist

And God said CREATE   Jan. 2, 1991

Science has shown that every animal carries in its brain and cellular makeup the memories of each preceding order of ancestor in the evolutionary chain, including stones and plants. Every proton in the Universe was present at the Cosmic Birth. All the potassium molecules in our bodies are radioactive because they were formed in the explosion of a star. You could say we carry star memory within our bodies. 'Memories' of animal ancestors are recapitulated during the development of the embryo of each species. In the ancient Upanishads of India it is written: "If you do not find it in your own body you will not find it elsewhere."

In addition to being a living record of preceding evolutionary stages, every animal has an overlay of behaviors appropriate to that particular species that are necessary for its survival. This overlay is called instinct. Instinct is a form of proscribed ritual. Instinct, added to behaviors learned from parents in the case of higher animals, is responsible for 'bearness' and 'chicadeeness' and 'dogness' etcetera, providing the animal with most of what it needs for survival in its companion environment.

In humans the overlay has a very small instinctual component. In its place is a very large capacity for learned behavior, much greater than any other animal. Even though humans learn a tremendous amount from parents, siblings, peers and elders, still the human imagination coupled with the DESIRE TO KNOW is not satisfied. We must, it seems, as individuals and as a species, create our own interface with our environment, create our own rituals for survival. Other animals' ritual interactions with each other and their surroundings are largely programmed by instinct, whereas a key characteristic of humanness is the necessity of creating our own niche in the world, and creating it over and over again because human culture never stands still.

And God said CREATE.

Perhaps the reason every culture has a creation myth as its central mythology is that the human behavioral instinct necessary for survival is the capacity to interact creatively with our environment. We come with no instruction booklet except what we learn. For us humans, *anything is possible*. The phrase that came to me during an Authentic Movement session so strongly I had to shout it, breathless, as from inside a dream, was this:

This body

is only limited

by the scope

of its Imagination.

Our task during this perilous chapter of the human story is to break the bonds of limits to the imagination, to break once again the container that has grown too small, so we can see more of the totality of the life we embody. In truth, we are infinity. How delightfully ironic that science, by separating, dividing and dissecting into ever smaller component parts has found its way around to the truth: the seamless interconnectedness of all things.

Shape-shifters, shamans and mystics throughout the ages have experienced oneness with animals, plants and elements, often as a rite of passage. The best tribal hunters become one with the prey. Since we contain within our cells memories of all of Earth's creatures and indeed of the essence of Gaia herself, we as humans may make the choice to bring into our consciousness an experience of other forms: stars, birds, fish, snakes, trees, wind, water, fire and earth. Scientists and shamans alike are telling us that the sounds, the movement, the awareness is already seeded in us. The stories of other life forms on Earth as well as of stars and galaxies far distant are inseparable from our own stories. They are part of us, they are our building blocks. We are part of their dream and they of ours.

Addiction to Things

My daughter saw something important one day when she was nineteen. She had been working with a Native drum maker turning animal skins, bones and feathers into drums and rattles. To make a beater for a drum she goes into the forest to find a beech tree, a branch of just the right width and flexibility. She gives thanks to the spirit of the tree, which becomes a partner in the making of a sacred object, as does the spirit of the deer whose skin she prepares by soaking, scraping and stretching. The finished drum will sing with the voices of deer, beech and daughter, united in the creative act.

What my daughter saw is that we have become a throw-away society because we have no connection to the things we buy and throw away. Our labor is very far removed from the origin of the goods we purchase. Perhaps money *is* the root of all evil in that it separates us from the act of creation. Perhaps that is why we are so hungry for 'things' and also why 'things' will never satisfy our hunger, because it is not actually things that we hunger for, but the feeling of meaningful creative connection to and interaction with Source that any human-made object implies. For every human-made object is the result of a human creative act. Some human being imagined the thing, interacted meaningfully with the source materials and had the satisfaction of creating something new. If it happens to be beautiful and useful, the satisfaction is even greater.

I propose it is this deep satisfaction of creating that is what we hunger for and try to touch by buying things.

Buying things, new things, gives us a connection to *someone's* creative energy. Someone created this thing, and we can get a piece of the magic by buying it. It is actually our own creative energy we are seeking, our own hunger for connection to Source via meaningful interaction with the raw materials of life.

Please recall that it is precisely this addiction to things that fuels our consumer economy, pollutes our planet, turns old-growth forest into newsprint so that each of us can have the thrill of buying second- or third- or thirty-fourth hand, someone else's creative energy.

Until we connect with our own creative energies we will not be satisfied. An aspect of the Wheel of Karma is surely the wheel of addictive buying and selling and throwing away.

Look around you. Is this true? Do you want to get off the addiction wheel? Where is your own creative energy? Where are your own source materials? How can you connect creatively with the source and stop our human addiction to things that is consuming our planet and our sanity?

i dis-cover my stories

unfurling like a colored ball of ribbons

with tiny precious surprises enwrapped

fluttering butterflies release as ball unrolls itself joy-fully

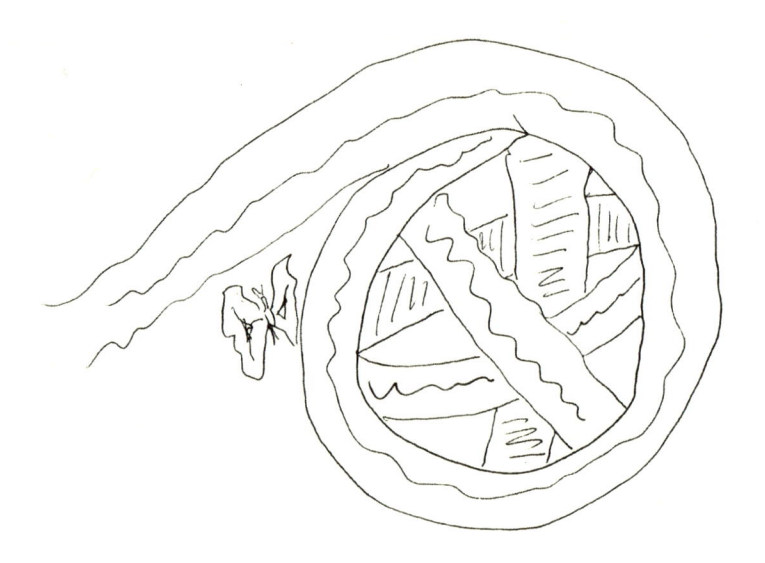

i become nakeder

Chapter Two:

Sonata to Eros

Introduction: Excerpt from "The Erotic as Power" by Audre Lourde

First Movement: "Freedom" - Con moto

Second Movement: "The Inner Lover" - Andante delicioso

Third Movement: "Fog Brain" - Lento

Fourth Movement: "Nocturne" - Presto

Fifth Movement: "The Mystery" - Adagio mysterioso

Introduction:

Excerpt from "The Erotic as Power" by Audre Lourde

The word 'erotic' comes from the Greek word *eros*, the personification of love in all its aspects, born of Chaos, personifying creative power and harmony. When I speak of the erotic, then, I speak of it as an assertion of the life-force of women; of that creative energy empowered, the knowledge and use of which we are now reclaiming in our language, our history, our dancing, our loving, our work, our lives...

The erotic is the nurturer or nursemaid of all our deepest knowledge...

Another important way in which the erotic connection functions is the open and fearless underlining of my capacity for joy. In the way my body stretches to music and opens into response, harkening to its deepest rhythms, every level upon which I sense also opens to the erotically satisfying experience, whether it is dancing, building a bookcase, writing a poem, or examining an idea...for once we begin to feel deeply all the aspects of our lives, we begin to demand from ourselves and from our loves' pursuits that they feel in accordance with that joy of which we know ourselves to be capable. Our erotic knowledge empowers us, becomes a lens through which we scrutinize all aspects of our existence, forcing ourselves to evaluate those aspects honestly in terms of their relative meaning within our lives."

~ Excerpted from a paper delivered at the Fourth Berkshire Conference on the History of Women, Mt. Holyoke College, August 25, 1978

First Movement: "Freedom" - Con moto

Allowing everybody to be just who they want to be.

You can go ahead and be that way if you want to.

It's okay with me.

I will be me and I LOVE being me. Being me feels SO GOOD.

Being me is laughing a lot and crying when I feel like it.

You can go ahead and do the same and it can be OKAY with me.

I am free and I want you to be free.

I am free and it feels so good.

I want everyone to be free to feel just how they want and I don't want to make us both feel not-free by desiring you to be or feel a certain way.

Some say "Repress thy neighbor as thyself."

Free thyself and thee won't want to repress anyone.

Nor force anyone to be free.

Second Movement:

"The Inner Lover" - Andante delicioso

non-genital auto-eroticism

polymorphic perversity*

perverse

perverse. Breakthrough.

"All acts of Love and Pleasure are My ritual."

"I couldn't eat my oatmeal on the last morning because I was feeling so one with everything, including oatmeal." Breakthrough.

Alone, writhing on sofa, head nuzzling into foam-covered cushion,

gurgling, spine spiraling delicious nearly orgasmic sensations

rolling with the movement

non-sexual erotic movements from the body-self to pleasure itself. to pleasure itself. itself. Movement not dictated, originating from the body-self who loves itself and wants itself to be free to enjoy. Alone. Not directed toward other or outer. Non-directed orgasmic erotic self-contained voluptuous self-fulfilling

Because. Because it feels good.

The body speaks freedom and pleasure.

the body loves itself

the body allows itself to move in ways which are solely for its totally personal totally selfish

polymorphic

pleasure

All acts of love and pleasure are my ritual.

Not because someone says "Here, this will feel good" nor in imitation of the instructor or because "it is good for you" or because you desire to be flexible or fit or tuned-up or to look a certain way or to have an orgasm or a sexual thrill or to release anything or to prove to yourself you can do it or to make you feel better or because it is not socially acceptable and you are rebelling

but because YOU LOVE YOURSELF.

The Inner Lover.

Freeing the Inner Lover.

A day. Give yourself a day when no one else is home. Meet your inner lover. Say hello and then agree to merge.

Come alive to the joy of BEING in a BODY.

This is an advanced exercise.

(*polymorphic perversity is a Freudian term for anarchistic and indiscriminate explorations of "all the erotic potentialities of the human body" or "the pursuit of pleasure obtained through the activity of any and all organs of the human body" including "the pleasure of touching, of seeing, of muscular activity, and even the passion for pain.")

Third Movement:

"Fog Brain" – Lento

It first hit in the spring of 1985. After a snowy winter at home with the kids, I took a temporary job helping at a friend's business. It was part-time, easy work with friendly people, a snap, I thought, and fun. I found it quite difficult. I found I could not take a phone message without effortful concentration. Alphabetizing files took three times as long as it should. My mind moved through seas of thick pea soup. Logical thinking became a supreme effort of will. Things I had been very good at for most of my 35 years, cheerful efficient organizing, remembering details, became next to impossible. Disturbed, I considered seeing a doctor but didn't know what I would say. After I'd been 'working' about a month, a death in the family changed our financial situation, so I had a good excuse to quit.

A few months later, in the garden at home my sacrum would slip out of place, starting me on an odyssey resulting in a major reorganization of my inner and outer experiencing of self in the world.

I now see the first fog-brain episode as a prelude to the coming changes, a clearing of the decks to make way for psychic reorganization. It has happened a number of times since, usually in conjunction with work that is no longer appropriate for me. Now a familiar friend, fog-brain helps me stay on target. When my ego thinks I can do something for money or fame, something involving skills the ego is attached to in some way, fog-brain says "Uh-uh. No way. Stop this fruitless nonsense and get on with your own work." Its most recent visitation came just before I began this book. A voice said, through the fog, "You can't do this job anymore." Chuckling, I gave notice the next day. At the same time, my private practice thinned to almost nothing. The decks were being cleared.

Adagio with pauses:

Fog Brain is for making space.
It is for un-gelling the old jello
clearing the mucky-way so the milk can flow again into new pathways.

Fog-brain makes space......

doesn't obscure anything......

is like cleaning house, ...

making space ......

for night teachings.

Opening......to......the......mystery.

Fourth Movement:

"Nocturne" - Presto

Night teachings:

The veil is lifted for a moment.
For a moment the flow is resumed
to and from the Source.
Too shocking in black-white clear-edged day light
to be absorbed by delicately interpenetrating realities,
dreams weave it together.
Re-weaving the threads
is like re-programming the computer: the neurons dance apart
re-shuffle
and take a while to gel into the new configuration.
Soul food.

Fifth Movement:

"The Mystery" – Adagio mysterioso

When we cough, do we understand why we cough and how we cough? No. We just do it. Same for digesting food or smelling roses or clearing our throat. It happens and we don't think anything of it because it is our bodies doing what they naturally do.

What is the nature of consciousness anyway? Is it what we choose to think about? Ten percent of our brain is used in ways science understands. The rest is unknown. It happens, whatever it is, in spite of not being known by us and our science, although science is working hard at expanding our knowledge. We currently have a tiny peek into causality and a tiny peek is probably all we can survive knowing at this time. Perhaps now we are opening to another ten percent. I really hope so.

A recent discovery in astronomy is that ninety percent of the matter in the Universe is 'dark' matter and it is somehow responsible for the ten percent we can account for. It holds it in place and right now we haven't the foggiest idea how, or what it could possibly be made of or anything much about it except that it exists out there and there is nine times more of it than the familiar light-reflecting matter. Although it can seem somewhat shocking to think of dark matter, it is clearly not a new thing at all. Now that we know that it is out there, *we want to know* more about it!

Humans emerged from animal consciousness into human because we want to know. Because we want to know, we have gradually come further into the Revealing Process. We want to see the process by which we come to know that which we want to know. It is natural and inevitable, in a way, that a desire expressed by us moves the Revealing Process in the direction of the desire.

> The wheel turns itself
> in a desire to feel its own motion
> and by so feeling,
> to know itself in a new way.
>
> The process is the mystery.
> We are the process.
> We are the mystery.

We do not understand the process we are in because that would involve standing outside of it. Opening to it is the appropriate attitude. Say out loud, right now, "I am open to being Mystery in Process." How does it make you feel to say that? Or try this one: "I am Universal Mystery in process right now." Or "I am the unfolding flower of Universal Consciousness." Can you let yourself merge with the truth of it? Or do you still have to separate – is it still too scary? That's okay. It takes a while to sink in.

Chapter Three

Development of a Species

<u>Tracing the Development of Human Consciousness</u>

Watching a child grow

In the womb, all is provided. In the womb the child has no sense of self, no sense of wanting, only the slow dream of growing to fulfill the orderly plan of sperm and egg. Begun in pleasure, planted with love, the embryo has only to manifest its blueprint.

Birth – a shock. The warm womb becomes too small, and one day the fetus is being squeezed and pinched and forced to slide down a very cramped passageway to who knows where...

Suddenly AIR and LIGHT and LOUD NOISES. The child is born.

With the exception of the past 60 years or so in the 200,000 year history of homo sapiens, **childhood** is spent mostly with Mother. Ideally it is a safe, peaceful time of gradual steady growth, of learning basic skills such as walking, talking, and learning by playing. The childhood arena is the home, and home is where the family is, where the mother is.

Until **puberty**. Sex hormones begin to be produced, changing the child's body into an adult's. For a girl the changes are gradual, but for a boy the hormones can 'hit' during a forty-eight hour period – WHAM! And suddenly all his wiring is changed. Confusion, exhilaration, physical and emotional awkwardness. Puberty can cause a violent break from the child's peaceful world of mother, home, family.

Adolescence lasts nearly ten years in our culture. It is characterized by experimentation, rebellion, egotism and exploration away from home. For boys especially it is a difficult time as they seek to define their newfound manhood by getting away from the influence of the feminine, especially away from Mom. Boys' rights of passage often involve life-threatening situations. In traditional cultures adolescent boys' rituals, although risky, are set up by the older men and are culturally sanctioned. Today our teens must invent their own rites of passage. Many choose drugs or fast cars or gang wars, all of which clash with our established sense of law and order and serve to increase the adolescent's sense of alienation from the main culture. Traditionally, girls' passage into adulthood required not so much a break as an acceptance of responsibility for continuance. For both sexes adolescence is a time of accelerated learning, and challenging expansion of self into the world.

The passage into the next developmental stage, **adulthood**, is traditionally marked by marriage, the sacred covenant joining the pair of opposites in order to bring forth and nurture new life. If puberty and adolescence can be characterized as breaking away on an outward trajectory, marriage can be described as closing the circle to bring the energy generated on the outward adolescent journey, back into and down toward the new home. In marriage both partners agree to harness their creative energies in service to life as it is represented by their own children.

The history of human consciousness has followed a path analogous to the development of the individual. The historical and pre-historical periods can be characterized as follows:

WOMB: 4,500,000 to 40,000 BCE ~ Transition from apes to humans (Africa)

- first tools/art are bi-faced 'hand axes'
- in the womb of humanness; dream-like; an unconscious growing away from animal consciousness into human consciousness
-

BIRTH: 40,000 to 10,000 BCE ~ Upper Paleolithic Age (Europe)

- explosion of cave art; 'birthday celebration'; becoming self-aware; explosion into celebration of human consciousness;
- hunter-gatherers – seasonal migration

CHILDHOOD: 10,000 to 3500 BCE ~ Neolithic Age (Europe)

- age of the Great Mother Goddess
- slow, orderly growth, safe and steady
- learning of culture-crafts and other basic skills
- focus on family, home and nurture
- cooperative
- no evidence of weapons or war
- agricultural, settled in one place

PUBERTY: 3500 to 2000 BCE ~ Bronze Age (Europe and Middle East)

- shocking invasions by men on horseback; sudden shock-waves (testosterone rush?)
- break-up of settled, peaceful agricultural life

ADOLESCENCE: 2000 BCE to 2000+ AD   Patriarchal Era

- outward looking; self-important; irresponsible to home
- characterized by exploration, experimentation, rapid change
- little respect for what went before
- competitive, risk taking

- industrial, technological

ADULT: 2000 to ??? Marriage and Family
- can we do it?
- maturation, wisdom, responsibility
- conscious relationship to the whole; taking care of all members
- Partnership respecting and recognizing strengths as well as weaknesses

Journey of a Species

The <u>embryo</u> of human consciousness develops in the womb of darkest Africa. We emerge gradually from the dream of the animals into the birth of a sense of humanness apart from animals. We celebrate the birth of our species' identity by illustrating and enacting our new sense of place in the universe with a joyous explosion of magical art. Sacred consciousness and human consciousness are born together, art being the natural expression of the two-in-one emerging, inseparable.

Our <u>childhood</u> was spent with the Great Mother, safe within the home and family consciousness of Neolithic times, a time characterized by slow growth and accumulation of basic culture skills including agriculture, cooking, metallurgy, animal husbandry, writing, math, building, pottery and so forth. The peaceful character of this seven thousand year epoch is attested to by the fact that the cities were not walled and neither were they built upon easily defended hilltops. Puzzled at first, archaeologists with the help of such free thinkers as Marija Gimbutas have concluded that Neolithic cities were not fortified *because there were no wars.*

Feminine consciousness in humans develops first, in the lap of the Great Goddess. She had her full say during a glorious period that personified all the best in woman: her ability to safely nurture all forms of life. She was so successful that she created overabundance in the form of extra humans (cities) and extra goods (grain surpluses) that led to her downfall as men began to be needed for organization and protection of the stores of surplus grain.

Masculine consciousness broke out like pimples on the <u>pubescent</u> face of humanity, when men on horseback invaded from the north (although the Hebrews invaded on foot from the south) shattering our stable woman-centered family. To feel itself separate from femaleness, <u>adolescent</u> male psychology had to ignore and repress the feminine in itself. Being by nature immature, it projected its fear of its own feminine qualities onto convenient scapegoats, members of our species whose bodies personify femaleness, namely women.

Women were repressed and feared as masculine consciousness flexed its newfound muscles, prancing about declaring itself to be God. All of the natural characteristics of maleness were elevated and those of femaleness devalued.

Masculine qualities have flourished over the past several thousand years in the form of philosophy, technology, science, commerce, war, conquest, and exploration. It's been a thrill, guys, but it is coming to a necessary end as our planet becomes overpopulated from too many wild oats, and polluted from an excess of *bull*-shit, a common byproduct of technology and competition.

Right now we are at a pivotal time in the history of our species and of the planet. The next stage in our development must be the move into responsible adulthood. The pendulum, having fully swung in one direction during the Neolithic, has swung fully to the other during the Patriarchal. We are poised at the turning point.

Continuing in the same arc is not possible. Our earth, our beautiful home, is telling us THIS WAY WON'T WORK ANYMORE. The feminine is needed to balance the excess of masculine in our culture. But, as with the 20-year-old who may dream nostalgically of childhood or teenage adventures, we cannot go anywhere but forward into our lives. What is next for the young adult as well as for us as the human species, is to become mature responsible adults, mature men and women, equal but different partners, both necessary for their contributions to the new life we will create together, as well as responsible for the repair of consequences of our thoughtless actions during adolescence.

"The historical mission of the present is to introduce a more integral period of earth development, a period when a mutually enhancing human-earth relationship might be established – if indeed the human is to prove itself to be a viable species on a viable planet."

~ Thomas Berry

Marriage is the symbolic passageway into adult consciousness, in this case a marriage of the inner feminine to the inner masculine, a covenant signaling acceptance of responsibility for continuance of healthy family life.

What are the characteristics of the healthy family? The healthy family is not about power-over. It is not about denial, it is not about coercion, nor is it about competition. The business of the healthy family is not to repress one member so another can flourish, but to encourage, support and balance the lives of all of its members so that all may experience an abundance of joy and happiness. For four thousand years our species has encouraged human male adolescent psychology at the expense of everyone else, including forests, oceans, and animal life as well as women, children and anyone in need.

Space exploration has brought poignant evidence that we are One Earth family, but we are a dysfunctional family in recovery from Western civilization.

The Universe Story and chaos theory tell us the history of the universe is characterized by a series of irreversible transformations that could not have been anticipated by having knowledge of what went before. We are surely on the threshold of one of those irreversible transformations. All you fish out there, get ready to breathe air.

~~~

The remainder of this chapter consists of an exposition of the timeline content, written by Peter Adair, my beloved. Together we developed the timeline, based a great deal on Peter's study of human history. **It is a history lesson**, written in Peter's voice. I am including it because it clarifies the progression from Womb to Maturity that is outlined above. If you don't want to read a fascinating excursion into history and pre-history, you can skip ahead to Chapter Four.

Prehistoric and Historic Archetypal Male/Female Relations
Peter Adair

Forest and Savannah Primates

Our human history begins in our pre-history, 5 to 7 million years ago, when we humans-to-be split off from the forest primates, our nearest relatives. Primate societies, particularly those of chimpanzees (who have an active genetic structure 99.6% identical to that of humans), reveal the basic social structures and male-female patterns of relating that were prevalent before our ancestor primates were forced from the forest.

There are two chimpanzee species: common chimps and bonobos (also called pygmy chimps), a later branching from the main chimpanzee line. Socially, the differences between these two species could not be more stark.

Primates led by males: Chimps

Tree-residing chimps live within a hierarchy of dominance and control, status and ranking. There is a great deal of competition and aggression to determine the alpha male, one of whose privileges is to be first in line when the females are in estrus (heat). The principal interactive way adult male chimps relate to females is during estrus for a perfunctory fifteen-second copulation.

Primates led by females: Bonobos

In contrast, bonobos, who spend much of their time on the ground walking upright without support of their knuckles, live in a society that is female-centric, with males neither dominating nor leading. Unlike chimps, there is no hunting, infanticide or killing of males by males. There is no obvious hierarchy, and friendly feelings between males and females allow for large groupings.

What engenders such a radical difference in social structuring, especially in male/female behavior, among species that are virtually identical?

The female is the key. Bonobo females have loosened their ties to the estrus cycle: they are eight times more available for mating than chimp females. Sex is used deliberately as appeasement to reduce tensions within the group. Since sex is no longer used solely for reproductive purposes, and is more frequently available, males do not compete aggressively for favors, and large cooperative groupings are possible.

Human females do not have an estrus cycle. Sexual availability of human females is completely divorced from reproductive demands. This condition is unique among animals, except perhaps dolphins.

Five million years ago, those primates who were to become our ancestors were forced by climatic change or some other social or environmental condition, out of the shrinking forest into the alien and hostile environment of the open savannah, where lurked the deadly cats of Miocene Africa. How were these unlucky, vulnerable, ill-adapted creatures able to survive in such a harsh habitat?

Our ancestors survived by means of two unprecedented evolutionary innovations:

1. In the female, the disappearance of the estrus cycle and the appearance of a menstrual cycle based upon the phases of the moon. As with bonobos, greater sexual availability fostered greater group bonding and cooperation, which was absolutely essential in maintaining the social group and insulating the life-generating females and their young from danger. Sex then became a multi-purpose activity used for emotional and social bonding, pleasure, communication and comfort. *"The human race was definitively shaped by the capacity of the female for non-reproductive sex."* - Sjoo and Mor

2. In the male, the development of a predator consciousness, after what was a long period of being defenseless prey for the big cats.

The Upper Paleolithic – The Garden of Eden

The Upper Paleolithic is the time of the great cave paintings and the earliest of the goddess figurines, from 40,000 to 10,000 years ago. It is a period when men and women were valued equally by the culture they co-created, a feature common to all hunter-gatherer groups. This period saw the blossoming and expression of sacred consciousness, as human consciousness began differentiating itself from the world around it. The cave paintings show a joyous explosion, a celebration perhaps, into art that expresses our newly born human awareness.

Hunt Magic and Moon Magic, Myths of the First Humans

Using the available evidence, we can imagine the myths our forebears told themselves about their relationship to Nature and their world.

The two primary myths, one for men and one for women, are Hunt Magic and Moon Magic.

Hunt Magic

Men bonded as hunters in sacred relationship to their world through the mystery of the animal hunt. The hunt called forth unique masculine capacities, skills and strengths, as hunting teams cannily used their intellects to anticipate and outsmart prey, to create traps and make weapons. The shaman, a traveler among the spirit worlds of men and animals, was the embodiment of the mystical, life-vitalizing relationship between those who killed and those offering their animal beings to be killed. Men recognized their place as protectors and providers, in relation to the life-giver, the woman.

Moon Magic

The Goddess in Paleolithic society is mistress of animals and is associated with women whose bleeding and birthing conjoins with the moon's phases. This mysterious correspondence is marked by the first expression of time-factoring: thirteen marks on a crescent horn, the root of our analytical/mathematical understanding of the world. (See *Venus of Laussel*, p. 48) Woman is also gatherer of up to 70% of the group's food in the form of plants. Woman is the maker of human beings and through her creative nurturing relation to her offspring, the introducer of food sharing, affectionate bonding and speech.

The Paleolithic is a time of balance. Males bond in groups in sacred relation to the world outside themselves, a bonding calling forth their masculine powers and abilities in service to, and in protection of, the life-generating mysteries of woman. Women's fertility cycles linked the earth with the heavens; her body was the locus for all human evolution.

The Mesolithic

The era of the Paleolithic recedes as the animals that were its unifying center become scarce. The Mesolithic is a transition time: a rending of the wholeness of the Paleolithic by a deep splitting of the fructifying interplay of the male and female capacities. Separately there now develops:

1. Plant breeding from the gatherers, and the transition to settled living by relying upon the life-sustaining fruits of plants, initially collected and then seeded. The Moon Magic of the women who were *plant-gatherers*, now becomes a magic of *plant-growers*, as the female develops the horticultural into the agricultural. The development of agriculture gives rise to the Neolithic era.

2. Animal breeding from the hunters. A culture of hunter-nomads develops in pursuit of diminishing game. Hunt Magic is lost, transmuted into animal husbandry by herder-nomads. From the domestication of large

animals, an understanding of the male role in the generation of life – the production and insertion of the magical seed - is gained. This seminal knowledge is one of the germs of patriarchal culture.

The Neolithic: Age of the Great Goddess

The Neolithic era sees the apotheosis of goddess power. Women predominate as inventors of agriculture and culture crafts, while men become for a time sedentary farmers. The Neolithic period is the heyday of the Great Goddess, Mistress of Heaven and Earth (through her connection with the moon), as well as Mistress of Animals who came from her womb, as illustrated by the cave artists of the Paleolithic. During the Neolithic, the Goddess also becomes Mistress of Plants. In addition she is midwife of pottery, metallurgy, weaving and food processing (cooking). All of the fundamental culture crafts composing the foundation of what is called civilization are innovations developed by the female. In Neolithic society, all facets of the Goddess' life cycle are recognized, including the paradox of the complementary light-and-dark aspects of existence. The full, fecund energy and consciousness of universal woman is elaborated in this time of matrifocal culture.

During the Neolithic, the male psyche that for hundreds of thousands of years found its numinous niche as the hunter in hunter-gatherer bands, is submerged. No longer is there purposeful male bonding for an activity through which the male could define himself. Although there were male roles in farming, these were not male bonding experiences, because agriculture was a creation of the feminine psyche. After the Paleolithic balance, the female found a full range and expression of her powers within the agricultural society of the Neolithic era. This was not true for the male. Feminine power grew like a seed into a very large plant, as males were squeezed and kept from the sun.

The Neolithic is a period of imbalance expressing an excess of the feminine principle. It is a period of an overabundance of nurturing and a deficiency of the blade of discernment (of limits). Material overabundance takes the form of grain surpluses. No longer do the free gifts of nature suffice as adequate sustenance for humans. Instead, plant life is manipulated and surplus is produced.

Transition to Patriarchy – the Violent Bronze Age

Paradoxically, the agricultural success of the female-centered Goddess cultures gives rise to a male-dominant governing system. In the stable Goddess culture, women communed directly with others and Earth. However, when the web of sacred cohesion is stressed due to increasing specialization and complexification of society, brought on by population growth sustained by an abundance of food stocks and the creation of cities, men, who can better mediate within hierarchical structures, entered the scene……..as kings.

Settled societies now evolve a social structure governed by kings, who are considered representatives of Sun Gods. In contrast, nomadic cultures, tending to be more strongly patriarchal, evolve a social structure governed by kings seen as representatives of impetuous Storm Gods. Western patriarchy is born in the desert among the Hebrews, and on the northern steppes of the Old World among the Indo-Europeans. Hebraic patriarchy is perhaps the more severe form, because it was birthed in the harsher climate of the desert. These two nomadic groups invade the settled villages, as the Old Testament documents for the Hebrews. When the Indo-Europeans domesticate the horse, warfare and conquest become the signature expressions of the impetuous, violent and destructive storm gods they worship. Just as Neolithic Goddess cultures expressed an over-balance of feminine energy, so the Storm Gods, and the patriarchal system they uphold, express an over-balance of the masculine principle developed in isolation from the feminine.

When grain surpluses accumulate, men are needed to guard the bounty, and a new warrior class develops. Males once again find definition within a bonding group, this time for purposes of control of wealth and invasion of other settlements. This innovative physical expression of male strength and power gradually permeates the entire male psyche. Men's consciousness becomes differentiated at this time, and grows into its own. A new masculine self-awareness is born.

It is in the Bronze Age, in response to the oppression felt within the previous goddess culture, that men consciously begin to suppress women's power. Males now assert a power over life and death that had been exclusively the domain of the female for the previous five thousand years. Mortal men could not take over the birth function (Zeus tried by giving birth to Athena from his head), but they could dominate the birth-givers, particularly by controlling distribution of the life-sustaining grain. And they could assert their power over death by *killing*. Killing by the blade was a very masculine way of death, versus dying passively in the arms of the Great Mother.

Early Patriarchy: Sun Gods and Storm Gods

The character of early patriarchal society reflected the qualities of the dominant masculine Sky Gods, of which there were two types: Sun Gods as in Egypt, and Storm Gods such as were worshipped by the Vikings.

The Sun God of the settled cultures rules a precisely arranged planetary and star system, of which he is the focus. The king, as the Sun God's representative on earth, embodies the Sun God's predictable and constant ordering principle, lording over a strictly hierarchical society with the god himself at its center.

Storm Gods of the invaders are the deified energies of thunder, lightning and tempestuous wind. Societies ruled by Storm Gods are explosive, exciting, dangerous, destructive, explorative and fast-changing. The fundamental structure of all later historical cultures derives from these two primary expressions of early patriarchal society.

Patriarchal rule quickly establishes itself in a dominance/power/control orientation. Women, formerly holders of status and power, are marked as the chief threat to the new masculine system. The Mesolithic witnessed the domestication of animals, and the Neolithic the domestication of plants. "With Patriarchy comes the domestication of woman," writes William Irwin Thompson. In Patriarchal culture the spiritual and sexual capacity of woman is denied.

The pivotal evolutionary innovation brought forth through woman in that distant time when our ancestors were forced into the alien and hostile savannah, namely the development of a sexuality that fostered a relationship between males and females that was no longer solely for reproduction, but for closer emotional and social bonding, is denied during the Patriarchal period. During the Patriarchal era, masculine qualities of innovation, experimentation and exploration are developing fully, but the evolutionary advance in females that began our journey into humanness is confined and suppressed. Instead, there is a regression to the hierarchic social order of the common chimp.

From the female mode of being of the Neolithic, we pass to the male dominant societies of the Patriarchy. The female way of being evolves first. Matrifocal culture precedes Patriarchal culture. Intriguingly, our biological evolution mirrors the evolution of human society. In the uterus, for the first two months after conception male embryos are virtually indistinguishable from females. The embryo will continue development as female unless altered by introduction of the male hormone.

> *"The female course of development is, in a sense, biologically intrinsic to all mammals. It is the pattern that unfolds in the absence of any hormonal influence. The male route is a modification induced by secretion of androgens from the developing testes."*
>
> *~ Stephen Jay Gould*

The human experiment is one of maturation. Culturally, the baton of evolution is held first by women, overwhelmingly so, via the development of menstruation, language, pottery, affectionate bonding, agriculture. The list is long. The baton passes to men when Patriarchy arises, allowing for freedom of exploration of the male mode of being. Males are a more recent and fragile biological development than females, which may help explain why male-centric culture is more difficult to establish in a positive way, than was the older, more stable female-centric culture.

The distortions of Patriarchy arise from *immature* expression of the male psyche. The *mature* expression is personified by kingly qualities of centering and ordering, exploring and experimenting. However, these qualities have rarely been achieved on the societal level. In early kingship we can witness *boy psychology* at work. The king is the embodiment of the son-lover of the Goddess, maintaining his connection with the mother, holding the sacred mandate by linking society with the cosmos (just as the female, in previous ages, held the link between human and heavenly bodies). Historically, he is a representative of gods such as Tammuz, Osiris and Dionysus.

When invasions by nomadic herders on horseback inaugurate the period of later kingship ruled by Storm Gods, we see the introduction of *adolescent male psychology*. This is the era of warrior-kings and empire building, of Sargon and Alexander, when the lure of excitement, danger, conquest and mastery are paramount. No caretaking element is involved in these dynamic expressions of the male adolescent.

Unlike the life of woman, revealed through a natural cycle or events such as menstruation and motherhood with their concomitant psychological and physical changes, the development of a man's life is not expressed through such clear and purposeful natural delineations. Men can become fixed in a particular orientation, unwilling to acknowledge or develop into other growth stages. Although kingship has historically fallen short of its promise, it is at least an archetypical evocation of integrated male energies and the fulfilled male life cycle.

The King is the archetypal expression of the mature masculine psyche, the king who has become a man, and is neither a boy nor an adolescent. The development of the mature king archetype is the male task.

~ W. I. Thompson

Kingship

In the late Neolithic there develops two kinds of kingship, each reflecting the natures of the Sun and Storm Gods. The former is a *sacred kingship* arising out of goddess worship (Osiris, Tammuz, Dionysus). The Sun God's king is the representative of the consort of the Goddess. He is her son and lover, steward of Earth's riches, which belong to Her. Gradually he evolves from being an expendable king-for-a-year into a permanent ruler, as trade, wars and cities grow beyond a woman's comfortable sphere of influence. At the same time, there is greater emphasis on individual personhood, the king being the embodiment of an *individual* life as opposed to a collective one. In a psychological sense it is the movement of the boy separating from his mother.

The sacred kingship of the Sun God differs from the kingship of the Storm God in the following ways:

Sacred Kingship : Sun Gods	**Secular Kingship : Storm Gods**
married to the land	married to accumulating wealth
to benefit the people	to exercise power, receive glory
agricultural society	nomadic herders, raiders
based on working the land	based on stealing from those who work the land

mystical go-between	material procurer of goods
boy psychology	adolescent psychology
magical	military

A sacred king embodying Dionysus, as the son and lover of the Goddess, personifies desire, joy, aggression and destruction as they manifest in the cycle of life. As long as he connects with the Goddess, he embodies the ever-dying and reborn power of life. Masculine gods of death and rebirth were personified in pagan Europe by the Green Man as the spirit of the grain that was cut down in the fall, reseeded to return green again in the spring, as well as the Horned God, Cernunnos, who was both the hunter and the hunted. When the male principle becomes separated from the Goddess, frozen into an individualized – and isolated – kingship, aspects of joy and rebirth are lost, and only those of aggression and destruction remain. The king loses his sacredness, and the Patriarchal society of which he is the center becomes imbalanced, distorted and diseased.

The ideal of the mature masculine kingship as expression of the mature masculine mentality was only rarely achieved in history. King Ashoka of India who reigned from 268-232 BCE is one example. Embracing Buddhism after winning his empire, and lamenting the human cost, Ashoka subsequently supported religious orders, built monasteries and shrines, issued edicts promoting tolerance and concord, and fostered the wellbeing of his countrymen and women.

In the West, the King Arthur legend is representative of the ideal, but it is a flawed example. Arthur is unable to successfully unite with his wife, produces no offspring, and is betrayed. Subsequently his kingdom becomes a wasteland, to be restored only by locating the Holy Grail (the feminine principle).

Witnessing Arthur without the Grail makes clear that the king principle cannot exist healthily in a separated, isolated condition. Just as a warrior requires a king to offer his services to, lest his warrior energies become misdirected, disoriented and therefore destructive, so a king isolated from the feminine principle is without foundation and sacred mandate, and therefore rules a kingdom that is a wasteland. This is precisely the condition of our evolved Patriarchy today.

The masculine principle (as represented by the king) is released from the isolation of Patriarchal expression when it connects with the Holy Grail, a chalice representing the feminine principle. This isolation may have been necessary at one stage in order for him to determine his selfhood. However, the king only becomes the manifest expression of the complete male form by embracing the life-enhancing principle embodied in the land, the anima, the woman. Then, and only then, does the masculine energy of kingship become once more life-affirming and sacred.

Chapter Four

Through a Doorway: Moon Magic and Hunt Magic

Did you know?

Did you know that in spite of the fact that the sun is four hundred times larger than the moon, and 92,700,000 miles further away, when seen from the earth the moon and sun appear to be <u>exactly</u> the same size?

Did you know that despite seasonal swings, over a one year period no matter where you live on the planet, the total number of minutes of day light will equal <u>exactly</u> the number of minutes of darkness?

Did you know that two days each year, on the Spring and Fall Equinoxes, every place on the surface of Gaia experiences <u>exactly</u> twelve hours of day and twelve hours of night?

And of course you know that ***approximately half*** of all the human beings born have been female, and half have been male.

summer solstice

June 21

winter solstice

Dec. 21

equinoxes
March 20
+
Sept. 20

45

<u>Polarities</u>

Polarities need not be opponents.

day : night

hot : cold

sun : moon

in breath : out breath

men : women

Duality need not be seen as an evil to be overcome or transcended,

Nor conflict as something to be willed away.

Complementarity can be celebrated!

Duality is a dance between lovers or friends,

not the enemy of Oneness!

Oneness loves duality, embracing it

as twin babes in a hammock.

Moon Magic and Hunt Magic:
Spiritual expression in the Old Stone Age
Upper Paleolithic Era: 40,000 to 10,000 BCE

> *In the Blood of Eden lie the woman and the man,*
> *the man in the woman and the woman in the man.*
> *In the mud of Eden so we end as we began,*
> *The man in the woman and the woman in the man.*
> *It was all for the union,*
> *Oh, the union of the woman, the woman and the man.*
> ~*lyric from "Blood of Eden" by Peter Gabriel*

This man-woman thing, we've been working on it for a long time. Our species has probably been trying to figure it out since before we left the trees. Peter and I knew early on that it would be part of our work together to figure some of it out. I'd like to share the piece about sacrifice and the spiritual path, to show how our earliest ancestors may have expressed the essential spiritual/ biological relationship of the sexes, so you can begin to see how the sacred drama between men and women has played out through the ages and into the present.

First there is what we call Moon Magic and Hunt Magic, women's and men's blood mysteries. The Moon Magic/Hunt Magic material is central to an understanding of all later gender-related spiritual expression because it establishes a baseline at the birth of humanity. It helps us understand that *from the beginning* men and women have had equally important but qualitatively different relationship to the divine.

> *"The boys' Rite of the First Kill and the girls' Rite of the First Menstruation are their respective rites of passage to maturity."*
>
> ~*Joseph Campbell, describing the Kung Bushmen of the Kalahari Desert, South Africa*

Venus of Laussel, c.25,000 BCE, 18" high
13 marks on the crescent moon horn, the first calendar
Carved in the rock just outside one of the Paleolithic initiation caves

Moon Magic

Moon Magic is women's blood mystery.

The locus of *Moon Magic* is the woman's body.

Moon Magic is *natural* in that it happens by following natural unconscious bodily rhythms.

Moon Magic is *passive* in that one is not required to 'do' anything other than follow the natural rhythms in order for it to happen.

Moon Magic sets up a numinous connection between women and the moon, whose cycles are synchronized naturally and effortlessly.

Sacrifice for the female involves surrender to the natural cycles of her life as she gives the totality of her physical and emotional being to the nurturance of her children and other loved ones.

Moon Magic is for women only. All women have it, it does not have to be earned.

Moon Magic rituals are menarche, menstruation, lovemaking (shared with men), childbirth, menopause.

Moon Magic's deity is the moon herself and the Great Mother.

The First Women

A little girl is growing and changing:
her breasts swell, her hips swell
she bleeds from down low
 her moon-wound bleeds but she does not die.
She bleeds when the moon is full,
and when it is not
the yearning sweetness of sex
brings the first taste of divine honey.
Soon her young breasts fill with milk and her belly rounds with life.
For nine moons she waxes
and on the tenth
she spills her secret.
Waves of love for the tiny new being pour from the heart of the girl-
woman
whose body brought it forth.

Initiation

"This is my baby.
From my body and blood was it formed.
My body swells and changes like the moon.
My body gives me ecstasy during love-making.
My body gives ecstasy to the men I take into it.
My body gives birth to tiny new beings
perfect and complete.
My body feeds the tiny ones their perfect food –
sweet milk from soft breasts.
My body cares for and nourishes the future of my kind.
My body is a miracle."

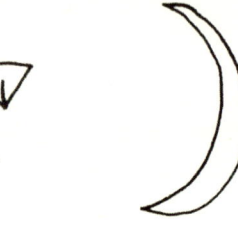

Woman
"I am woman.
My body is sacred.
Taking the sacred seed inside me, I gestate new life.
The moon herself grows in my belly.
My sacred blood is shed for birth, for continuance.
Yet with every Birth I face Death.
It is woman's way
to confront the mysteries of Death and Birth simultaneously,
accepting what is given.
Children are given and taken away;
my body comforts the sick and dying;
my body comforts and gives pleasure to the hunters, the men
who laugh with us, who bring us meat and songs
and protect us from the dangers of the night.
I know the ways of survival.
I know the ways of love."

The Wise One
"Grown older, my sacred body is wrinkled now,
a skin bag hanging on bones.
In my turn
I become the Wise One
sharing with my people the wisdom
of my moon-blood which is no longer shed:
knowledge of plants gathered for food and for healing,
songs for birthing and for passing over.
Telling and retelling the stories of my people
like the waning moon
I empty myself
preparing for rebirth."

(Hand-drawn symbols are from paleolithic artifacts.)

Sacrifice ~ Women's Way

Sacrifice for women involves surrender to the natural function inherent in the reproductive cycle. Physical and emotional suffering are implicit in childbearing, childrearing and attending to the ones you love. Love is biologically programmed into a woman's life by way of her second heart, her womb. Surrendering to love and its natural extensions provides woman with plenty of life-long opportunities for sacrifice for the sake of her family as she attends to the *personal* side of survival of the species.

Equal to Moon Magic is

<u>Hunt Magic</u>

> "When men go to the forest to hunt or fish, it is never a trivial passage. First the shaman must travel in trance to negotiate with the masters of the animals, forging a mystical contract with the spirit guardians, an exchange based always on reciprocity. The Barasana compare it to marriage, for hunting too is a form of courtship, in which one seeks the blessing of a greater authority for the honour of taking into one's family a precious being."
>
> ~from 'Peoples of the Anaconda', a chapter in <u>The Wayfinders</u> by anthropologist Wade Davis

Hunt Magic is men's blood mystery.

Hunt Magic is not a natural process, but must be attained through study, skill development and discipline, involving the intellect as well as the trained body.

In **Hunt Magic** the man's body is used as a tool in obtaining the goal; it is not in itself the locus of the mystery.

Hunt Magic involves active effortful pursuit of a goal.

Hunt Magic makes numinous connection between the hunter and the prey. The two become one during the hunt but the sacred oneness is rent by the act of killing the animal brother so that the human and his kind may have life. Because of the spiritual merging, the death of the animal brother (the prey) is felt piercingly by the hunter as a **sacrifice**.

In **Hunt Magic** the hunt itself becomes the sacred reenactment of the primal drama of emergence of human consciousness replayed thousands of times as early hunters cross and re-cross the thresholds between animal and human consciousness.

Hunt Magic rituals are: training of boys by men in the skills of the hunt; sacred initiation in the caves of the animal spirits; the hunt itself.

*The deity of **Hunt Magic** is the shaman, or shape-shifter, associated with the sun and with the lion (a solar animal), the bear or any animal with antlers.*

***Hunt Magic** is entered into for the benefit of the tribe.*

***Hunt Magic** establishes the association between men and violent death.*

It is crucial to our understanding of men's and women's spiritual natures that we see that the only possible balance to the miracle of giving birth (passively and naturally) is to take life (actively and intentionally) by killing.

<u>The First Men</u>
Sacrifice. My story I am telling.
I am hunter.
By my skill my people survive,
fresh meat gives life to us all.
First we learned to pick through carcasses left by the big cats
then to catch small monkeys
to cook over our fires.
Into our camps came
sabre-toother tigers peddling black velvet death
in the moonless night.

Defenseless, many of our kind were taken,
the young and the old ones, unable to run.
Desiring to live, we learned to hunt tigers
substituting spears and cunning for claws and speed.
We learned to think like the animals we hunt.
We study their habits, anticipate their movements,
becoming so like them that even when we come near them in the hunt
if we are skilled
they do not sense "human" but one of their own.
    'graceful leaps of the ibex
        - my body leaps
    stealthy stalking silently
        - my body hides and creeps
    the killing stroke
        - I scream and strike
    the ibex falls, stricken
        - my body writhes, afraid
    death bleeds silently
        - i am still
    our Mother weeps for the death of Such Beauty
        - i weep for the death of Such Beauty
    Her hunger is stilled
        - my hunger is stilled
    life from death
    remorse is born amidst rejoicing
    i run howling through the forest
    my feet beating the earth in a rhythmic dance
    i stop, my cries comingling with my tears
    my body rejoicing in its live flesh-and-bloodness
    I am alive!'

My story I am telling.
The ibex and I are one. Hooved ones
give their lives so that the two-leggeds
may have food and skins.
Life for life,
the gift <u>must be respected.</u>
When the time is right the men enter the sacred cave,
womb of the Earth, Mother of All Animals.
In the womb-cave images of Spirit Animals cover the walls.
In the womb-cave we dance the stories of the ibex, deer, bison and horse,
brothers all
who have given their sacred body and blood.
In the deepest place we pray in gratitude to the horned God of the Hunt.
To the Mother we pray to be forgiven for breaking Her wholeness by killing.
Drumming on sacred skins with sacred bones,
we sing and dance in the timeless place
so that the Mother of All Animals and the God of the Hunt will smile on us
bringing forth abundant life for all,
        abundant life for all.
I am hunter.
My story I am telling.

(Hand-drawn symbols are from paleolithic artifacts.)

Sacrifice – Men's Way

> *"Meat is not the right of a hunter but a gift from the spirit world. To kill without permission is to risk death by a spirit guardian be it in the form of a jaguar, anaconda, tapir or harpy eagle. Man in the forest is always both predator and prey...Animals are potential kin, just as the wild rivers and forests are part of the social world of people."*
>
> ~ from 'Peoples of the Anaconda', a chapter in <u>The Wayfinders</u> by anthropologist Wade Davis

The notion of sacrifice involving a willing or unwilling sacred death is mainly a men's thing. It comes from the necessity of momentarily identifying totally with the animal that one is hunting. The figure of the shaman represents the merging, a shaman being a person who travels to other realms sometimes taking the shape and consciousness of animals in search of healing medicine for the tribe. The other evening I attended a lecture by a modern shamanic practitioner and author, Tom Cowan. Cowan maintains that trappings aside, the techniques of core shamanism are very easy to teach because shamanism is an encoded part of the human primal experience. He maintains that children easily tap into magical realms peopled by talking animals (Mickey Mouse, the Lion King, Aslan), imaginary friends, fairies, trolls and the like, and although all of us have access to these realms, rational thinking has closed the doors for most adults.

During the hunt, the hunter enters an altered state of consciousness, becoming one with the prey. He gets inside the consciousness of the animal he is hunting first by learning its ways, observing it for long hours from a distance until he knows the animal so well that he begins to think and move as if he were that animal. Imitative psychic merging by entering temporarily into the dream of the animal is the way of the best tribal hunters the world over. A friend tells of his joyous merging with fish-consciousness which allowed him phenomenal success on a deep-sea fishing trip while others' lines were slack, and of leaping through the forest to play with deer who were not afraid because he was, body and soul, tuned to their wavelength.

When the hunter is obliged to *kill* the animal he has psychically taken as a brother, he betrays an aspect of himself. In killing the twin the hunter has sacrificed part of his own identity. Herein lies the inner conflict: self against self; human nature against animal nature; Theseus against the Minotaur. Hence the notion of sacrifice of the blissful state of oneness with nature for the sake of survival of the tribe.

The idea of sacrificing the life of a brother/self for the sake of continuance of the group one belongs to has become embedded in the male psyche. The guilt experienced by the one who kills must be redeemed through ritual purification and prayer, including recognition by the tribe that the hunter has acted not out of selfish motive, but for the survival of his own kind.

Elements of the masculine drama are:

Rigorous training		excitement of the chase
Skill-development	}leading to{	blissful merging with prey
Intellectual development		betrayal and death
		atonement
		redemption

In the drama of the hunt we can see the centrality of 'sacrifice as sacred death' to the masculine spiritual experience.

The enormity of the act of breaking the wholeness of the fabric of creation by killing, makes *redemption* a crucial piece of the male drama. Through redemption the hunters could feel themselves reconnected to the tribe and to the larger circle of life's creation.

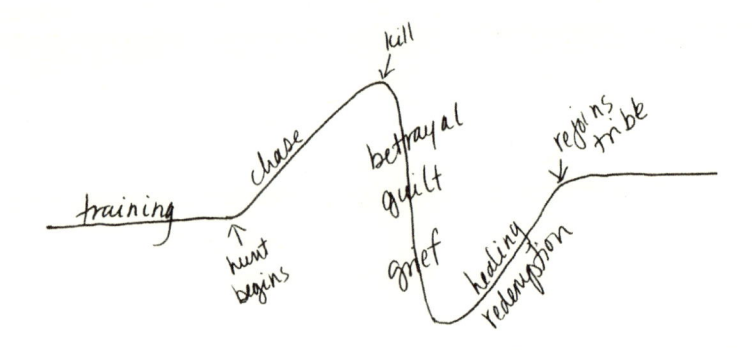

[Hand-drawn diagram showing an arc with labels: "training", "chase", "kill", "hunt begins", "betrayal", "guilt", "grief", "healing", "redemption", "regains tribe"]

(Peter points out how the shape of the masculine sacred drama parallels the drama of the male sexual organ.)

How the Men's Sacred Drama Has Played Out In The Different Eras

Paleolithic

In the Old Stone Age, bands of men hunted together, undertaking together the rigorous physical and spiritual training of boys.

The act of killing temporarily separates the successful hunter from the rest of the tribe necessitating a ritual *redemption*. In effect, he has 'sinned' for the sake of the tribe. Therefore the whole tribe is involved in 1) seeing that the individual hunter or hunters are ritually honored, purified and returned to the tribe physically and psychically intact, and 2) seeing that the spirit of the sacrificed animal is honored so that the Great Spirits will not be angered by a thoughtless act of aggression.

The return of the hunters to the bosom of the tribe (redemption) symbolizes the mending of the break in the fabric of life caused by killing an animal brother. The balance is restored. We may speculate that Paleolithic hunters were no doubt soothed by their women after their heroic adventures, literally being accepted once again into the bosom of the tribe. Participating in the life-*giving* half of the sacred blood mysteries by making love with women must have been reassuring and healing for the hunters after the drama and trauma of the life-taking hunt with its strong emotional mixture of elation and guilt.

Neolithic

In Neolithic matrifocal culture, male mysteries degenerated as the hunt was given up in favor of sedentary agricultural life-styles. The theme of male sacrifice and redemption was carried over into the yearly sacrifice of the sacred king, whose ritualized death atoned for the tribe's interference with the natural order, the interference in this case being the rearrangement of Nature's plan in order to allow for agriculture. Hunting still happened, but farming became the primary way of life.

Patriarchal

With the rise of masculine consciousness during the Patriarchal period, killing became primary again but without its sacred link to survival and food. This time the feminine mysteries were suppressed and all but forgotten.

Redemption was sought not by reuniting with the sacred feminine life-giving principle here on earth, but by unification with the heavenly father in Valhalla or Heaven. Redemption was postponed until after the death of the 'sinner'. Thus it was no longer possible for men to live in wholeness on this earth because they were not allowed to seek redemption in the original way, through reunification with the life-giving feminine principle. This seems a recipe for misery!

The Scapegoat

Famous scapegoats throughout history:

Philistines	Jews
Socrates	Injuns, Blacks, POC
Moors and infidels	drug addicts
Heretics	Feminazis
Witches	welfare mothers
Joan of Arc	LGBTQ

Once we see that during the patriarchal era it was not possible to be redeemed 'in this life' it is easy to understand how the game of scapegoating became so popular. Since it was not possible for sinners to be whole until after death (if then), and if one was by birth condemned to be a sinner living in a state of separation from the Divine (Christian doctrine of Original Sin) what was one to do with feelings of unworthiness and guilt?

One exciting and gratifying way to release pent-up energies of unredeemed guilt is to blame someone else, setting them up as the personification of the evil that one is feeling inside but is reluctant to ascribe to oneself, thus giving the individual and the society license to purge themselves of discomfort by attempting to wipe out 'evil' as it manifests *in someone else*. Finger pointing. Judging. Right and Wrong. A focus on 'Outer, Outer, Outer' because that way we don't have to look at the real source of the pain, which is 'Inner, Inner, Inner' and according to our (dominant Christian) beliefs, cannot be redeemed in this life.

> *Making others responsible for how we feel is the beginning of all violence, both internal and external, all conflict between people, and ultimately all wars between nations.*
>
> ~ Jeff Foster, <u>The Way of Rest</u>

There is a close parallel between the male version of sacrifice and scapegoating. Indeed, both are a variation on the same psychological pattern. In the Paleolithic, the drama of sacrifice was undertaken for the physical survival of the tribe. In the Neolithic, human sacrifice of the beloved year king (the lamb) was performed to propitiate guilt over interfering with Nature's plan. In the Patriarchal, the guilt was still there, but the victim moved from being 'one of us' to 'one of them', from lamb to goat, upon whom the group could project their collective guilt and get rid of it by expunging it. The scapegoat is killed (or hunted and reviled, in any case) in an attempt to restore emotional health to the group by cutting off the diseased part. In the Paleolithic the circle was made whole by *including and healing* the one who broke it (the hunter) but in the Patriarchal the circle is made whole by *excluding* the one who is seen to have broken it, inevitably forcing the circle to become smaller and smaller with an ever stronger 'us versus them' dynamic.

Note: Jesus played the double role of scapegoat (for the Jews who wanted him dead because he was a troublemaker) and sacrificial lamb (for the Christians whose sins he took away and redeemed with the Father in heaven). His drama, called The Passion, included in sequence all of the elements of the men's sacred drama: a long period of training and preparation, a three-year ministry where he merged with the people and was recognized, betrayed, suffered a bloody violent death on the cross, descended into Hell, and was resurrected, all for the sake of redemption of the group.

The Paleolithic hunt ended with a period of introspection and redemption serving to remind the men of their proper place in the circle. In the Patriarchic era the hunt takes on an open-ended character. Human 'enemies' real and imagined become prey in a domino game of conquest, violence and blame. Nurture of the family and the web of life is lost in pursuit of vainglory, spoils of war or the emptiest reward of all, revenge. In this century, corporate profits have become the highest goal, CEOs and billionaires the anointed ones, as everyone else and all of Nature is sacrificed in the name of accumulating wealth at the top.

Summary: Blood Mysteries

In the Paleolithic era of hunter/gatherer bands, equal respect was given to men's and women's blood mysteries. Both were essential to the continuance of the human species. In Western culture, masculine and feminine spiritual paths and powers have not been in balance since the Paleolithic ended in about 10,000 BCE with the shrinking of the large-animal population and the beginning of settled agriculture. It is interesting to note that two of the greatest threats to the survival of our species in the twenty-first century are caused by overwhelming success at *disconnected* manifestations of Moon Magic (overpopulation) and Hunt Magic (nuclear and other weaponry of war). Add to that the pursuit of corporate profits at the expense of people and planet, a distinctly Patriarchal goal, and you have the state of our current world crisis.

Now that technology has made possible the means to limit women's power to create human life, it seems appropriate that governments and religious leaders encourage women to do so for the sake of the survival of our species in its supporting environment. For the same reason it is appropriate that the masculine power to take human life through war and weaponry also be reexamined. Perhaps men's and women's energies need no longer be expressed in the old ways. Evolution is challenging us to drop the old forms, to express our essential natures via the whole self that is genderless, loving and creative. It remains to be seen whether we can let go of our gender bias and hierarchical habits of mind to move into a new and necessary vision embracing wholeness, cradling our complementary masculine and feminine natures like twin babes in a hammock.

'Oh, the union of the woman, the woman and the man'
~Peter Gabriel, "Blood of Eden"

Acheulean hand axe or bi-face

Mystery at Dawn

Acheulean Age: 1.4 million to 80,000 BCE

The Discovery of Beauty

'The fashioning of tools beautifully symmetrical and beyond the requirements of mere use, marks the beginning of the history of art already in the period of *Homo Erectus*. The pebble tools of *Homo habilis* and choppers found at Choukoutien can be explained – like the occasional tools of apes, in economic terms. Such an implement as the Acheulean hand axe, however, gives evidence of a grade of consciousness equal to satisfactions beyond the economic. Its size and the undamaged surface suggest an application to a symbolic function. Such an object of "divinely superfluous beauty" (Robinson Jeffers' phrase) may have served a ceremonial function. If so, the beginnings of ritual, as well as of art, must together be assigned (in Europe, at least) to the era of *Homo erectus*.' ~Joseph Campbell

"The Doorway"

For a long time I am in a small cozy room
I slide down a long narrow passageway
At the end there is a doorway
Passing through it I am changed

Acheulean so called 'hand axes' are said to have been the first human tools, beautiful objects created *by the thousands* nearly a half-million years ago, at an early stage in the emerging of human consciousness. I held one in my hand once. It was roughly the size and shape of my hand. Placing my palms on either side of it was like being palm-to-palm with stone-age people, two hands praying. For decades archaeologists have identified these beauties as hand axes, but microscopic inspection indicates little or no wear on the blade edges. Yet thousands have been found, often in piles near encampment sites in Europe, the Near East, India and Africa.

Bi-faces, as they are now called, were made (by men? by women?) by skillfully striking a flint pebble with another rock causing a large flake to break off the core. The flakes were used for cutting and scraping, but the elegant cores themselves are too large to have been practical. James Harrod suggests they may have been used only once, ritually, to cut meat. Joseph Campbell sees in this sublime shape "the birth of the spiritual life…of which the animals know nothing."

What is being signified here? Why this particular bilaterally symmetrical three-dimensional shape? What role did repetition of *this shape* play in the emerging?

Ponder these images:

the core emerging from the pebble

opposites: inner and outer

repetition, perfection, skill

"divinely superfluous beauty"

birth shape: doorway: vulva

hand-sized, hand-made

For me this shape represents one of the primary symbols of the psyche, that of birth in all of its manifestations, psychological, spiritual and physical. We have used this symbol, whether consciously or unconsciously, as doorways to our most holy places: churches, mosques and cathedrals. The Gothic arch mimics the shape of the Acheulean bi-face. Architect of sacred geometry Keith Crichlow says it is the shape of the etheric body. Creating this shape in stone or walking under a Gothic arch or in some cases simply by seeing this particular shape, we are symbolically crossing a threshold into some kind of rebirth. It is no accident that the threshold is shaped like a vulva, our first doorway into this life. Imagine pondering the doorway, creating the doorway *with one's hands* and in the process creating tools that will separate forever the humans from the animals. Imagine shaping the doorway over and over again, creating the symbol many more times than is practical because you are fascinated with the shape, the symbol of the new order of consciousness that we as a species are forming by the combined effort of hands and mind.

This is my take on it. What do *you* think?

It is a simultaneous experiencing of All Time, All Evolution, All Existence. We *are* Ceremonial time. *We are all of it.* Our role as humans is now and always has been to bring knowledge of what has always been, up into consciousness. This bringing up to consciousness is the thrust of science and history and philosophy and economics – to *know what is,* what has *always* been true, delving backwards into truth while simultaneously creating new interfaces, as though looking into a giant web stretching backward and outward that contains all natural phenomena, all history, all knowledge of what has ever been. We are beginning to see more and more of the web, the connections between all things, the universal laws. To be able to understand and therefore *to bring into consciousness* is the task, perhaps even the purpose of humans. We are the organ of consciousness of the earth. At the same time we are moving forward creating new reality. A thrilling, dynamic interface is the human.

Art is also relationship. Cave artists were perhaps exploring the numinous, magical and practical aspects of the relationship of humans to certain large mammals that must have symbolized something important to these early humans. Perhaps the portraying over and over of particular species was coupled with the realization of being different from animals in some qualitative way. There is lyrical rapture in this repetition, like being in love either with the animal or with the realization of difference, or perhaps in love with what the animal represents. There is a rapturous sense of *knowing something* that was expressed by painting or carving the symbol of the knowing over and over again. Above all there is a sense of YES! I *know this,* not as an empty cataloging of facts, but as a mystical merging with the new knowing and a birthing of the extraordinary creature that is the human being.

Art as a doorway into sacred numinous awareness is a knowing of another piece of the web that was there all along but the artist has not previously been aware of it. This is the magical transformative evolutionary revolutionary nature of art, and of science as well. This is the answer to "Why Art?" : to connect with another level of reality or consciousness that is beneath/above the surface layer of day to day reality that occupies us most of the time. Art personifies the growing of consciousness, a magical breaking through into KNOWING. The breaking through quality is true of all art forms. It is a potential of course that is not always reached, but it is the *why*, the source of and the impulse behind art, and it is, I feel, identical with "the sacred" in that through art, the artist and sometimes the observer/witness go beyond ordinary consciousness into other realities that have always been there but were previously unexperienced.

This is why art and the sacred are inseparable, and are essentially intertwined with the exploring ecstasy that characterizes the human species. **We want to know.** Cave art is the earliest expression of wanting to know, a taste of fathoming the mysteries, a recognition of something beyond instinctual survival awareness that we share with other animals. Cave art is the act of exploring and celebrating the magical relationship between the earliest humans and their environment, that mysterious interface between their inner and outer worlds that they could just then begin to express in symbol and story.

Two of 10,000 figures from Lascaux cave:

Paleolithic Art : A celebration of the Mysteries

The art left by our earliest ancestors is moving, indeed. Another magnificent cave was recently discovered in France, and we are looking forward to a renewed interest in deciphering the messages left by our ancestors of 40,000 years ago.

Moon Magic and Hunt Magic, men's and women's sacred blood mysteries, are illustrated by the following aspects of the earliest cave art:

Frieze of aurocks and horses from Lascaux Cave

Shaman of Les Trois Freres cave in France

Art related to Hunt Magic

- Rapturous repetitive portraits of selected large animals, primarily bison, deer, ibex and horse
- These are 'power' animals with numinous symbolic associations
- Painted or scratched on walls of initiation caves, sacred spaces akin to temples or cathedrals representing the womb of the Mother of All. A single figure of a shaman appears in the sanctuaries, or furthest recesses of the caves as if one meets the master of the hunt in the holiest of holies
- Shaman figures: eyes and face emphasized; body can be stick-like or animal-like
- Shaman of Les Trois Freres cave has horns on his head resembling Cernunnos or Herne the Hunter from Celtic myth
- There are no sculptural or realistic representations of the male human body

Venus of Willendorf, 4" high. Legs meant to be set into the earth

Art related to Moon Magic

- Sculptural forms of females
- Faces obscured or omitted, emphasizing reproductive function
- Large breasts, hips, thighs; pubic triangle emphasized
- Females are never painted, they are always formed from the material itself
- Relief sculptures are placed at cave entrances, never deep inside, indicating the feminine nature of the cave itself but not of its contents
- Small female figurines found in association with dwelling places; legs come to a point to allow them to stand upright in the soil indicating identification with the material of the earth itself
- Goddess of Laussel holds a crescent horn with 13 marks, her hand on her pregnant belly as if to say "See the association between the moon and my belly? I count 13 moons to the solar year. Counting comes from me."

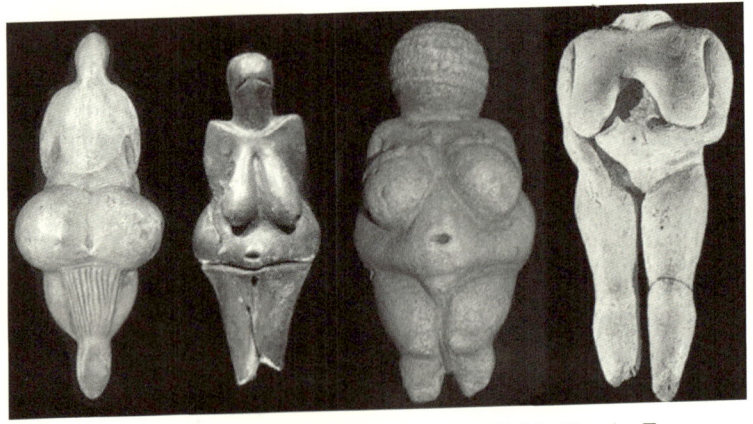

Small "Venus" figurines from the Paleolithic Era in Europe

Chapter Five

Under Her Skirts

the Silent Center
the She
the Soul
the Snake
the Serpentine
the Secret

the Soul, the Goddess Within
the Motivator
nay, the Motive.
the point from which
the Movement is initiated.

Note: the Deep She material was received in the middle of the night, as though channeled.

The Deep She – Part One

The Deep She
I surrender I surrender
She wakes me in the night
I surrender I surrender

She suffocates me with a dream:

I am diving into a lake but I can't get to the water. Can't breathe, can't swim, stuck on top of a layer of gel-like skin that's invisible until I try to be in the water as fish/human and I can't breathe and I can't swim. I feel VERY, VERY SAD

She tells me this:

'What would you say if I told you that you hold within your body the secret center of existence? And if I told you that you have <u>always</u> had this center of all-potential WITHIN YOUR BODY? It is like a secret organ that 'they', or perhaps 'we', have been hiding from us so that we will not know it and will not know ourselves. It is time for humans to begin to know ourselves again.

    Goethe wrote "Every object well-contemplated creates an organ of perception." Contemplate well so that you may come to know an organ of perception that is deep within your own body. For the natural seat of masculine consciousness is the head, but the natural seat of feminine consciousness is the body.

The Core

There are two aspects to our secret organ. The first is the 'core' that can be used to perceive emotions, energies and subtle realities of all kinds. It can be used for sorting, listening and picking up subtle clues as to the emotional truth of any situation. Imagining the core gives us a location in the body for (women's) intuition. Imagine a sensory organ starting at the throat going down to the perineum. It is cylindrical in shape, located just in front of the spine. The core is a receiving mechanism, not unlike a satellite dish or your outer ear. It perceives and recognizes momentary truths, picking up the emotional truth of any situation as it happens, in the now. Like the other five senses, the core gathers information for the benefit of the entire organism that can then be processed and stored elsewhere in the body.

Core knowing is the first part of the 'secret organ.' It is first because we re born with it, it exists in us and can be developed at any age. It is strong in very young children, who are usually taught to distrust it. It is usually stronger in women, but can be developed in men. Imagine if we went to school beginning at age five to develop this other type of knowing.

The Well

The second aspect of deep feminine knowing is like a cauldron or cup located between the uterus and the spine. You can find it by moving along down to the bottom of the 'core'. There you will find the 'well'. Down in the well it is always DARK, the true opposite of the masculine sun, light, God, etc. It is a dark place of waters, the seat of the *bindu*, the Hindu symbol of the seed of all-potential. It is the dark cauldron of ALL KNOWING, of ALL SHE-NESS, the damp dark center of existence. It is the seat of a woman's true power. It is near her reproductive organs, her creative center in that a woman creates human beings from her body.

"...whether or not a woman does conceive, she carries the germinative ocean within her, and the essential eggs. We have a spirituality, full from within. Whether we are weaving tissue in the womb or pictures in the imagination, we create out of our bodies." ~Meinrad Craighead

The well is a place of profound peace, a place of absolute knowing. It is a place of stillness out of which arises all things. On a symbolic level, all things that are of the material realm arise from this place in a woman's body, in *every* woman's body. It is maya, the ground of existence.

"The mother is abysmal space, a place. A hole, the hollow is hallowed and hallowed it heals. Here the holy dead are seeded in her dark matrix, take root and are re-membered."
~Meinrad Craighead

This place of power in her body connects every woman to the center of the earth. This place is the same vibration as earth, as low drumming, as the standing stones, as deep water, as whale song. This place resonates with ALL CREATION. "Everything was created out of Her body" is a profound mythical truth.

Imagine every woman on the planet connected to the center of the earth by a flexible stretchable cord from her deep center to the earth's center. This is how it is. This is how it always has been.

"Abwoon d'bah shimaya"

("Abwoon d'bah shimaya" is the first line of the Aramaic Lord's Prayer, translated by Neil Douglas-Klotz variously "O Thou, the breathing life of all," meant to be spoken or sung aloud. Try it.)

The Deep She: Part Two

Breaking Away

"Thou lovest them in thy heart; born of thee, born of thee."
-Hymn to a Moon Goddess written in 3400 BCE, Ugarit, Syria

The powerful psychic and mythic connection of Earth to Woman by their fiery centers was well known in the Neolithic Era, the Age of the Great Goddess. Toward the end of the Neolithic, men were likely struggling against overwhelming natural female power. It was the struggle of the adolescent boy to escape the magnetic field of his mother to become SINGULAR and MALE. It's never been easy. To break from being under the thumb, under the spell of the mother who knew what you needed before you knew it, who knew what you were thinking and feeling, who was connected physically and psychically to you, the child of her body, the child of her heart.

Remember the Neolithic son-lover kingships of Dummuzi and Osiris? Both were god-kings by virtue of the fact that they were lovers with their all-powerful mothers.

Imagine the awesome power of women in a culture where all children lived with their mothers *all of their lives*, where all property belongs to her, where men's role in making babies was known but valued mainly for his genes and not his ability to support a family or be a good father to his children, social fatherhood being unnecessary in those days.

Imagine the revolution, the bloody revolution that overturned the all-powerful Mother. Rape. Pillage.

Disregard for sacred groves, sacred places, for the houses and cities, for the things belonging to the Mother. Especially disregard for human life, her ultimate creation. And all to break the hold of the mother over the son SO THAT THE SON COULD GROW INTO A MAN.

He created a Father in heaven for himself, having no actual models for the role. A father-in-heaven who would be opposite to the mother-on-earth:

> demanding where she is permissive
>
> rule-oriented where she is flowing
>
> non-sexual where she is very sexual
>
> ascetic where she is sensual
>
> exclusive where she is inclusive
>
> hard where she is soft
>
> vengeful where she is forgiving
>
> wrathful where she is loving.

And on the side of the men. Definitely on the side of the men.

She tells me I am finished. It is 4:30am.

Chapter Six

Sacred Sex

Coming Out from Behind the Wall of Lies

A teen in the 1960s, I lied to my parents about sex. I felt obliged to lie to them, to feel ashamed.

Teenage commandments:
1. Thou shalt be ASHAMED of thy most pleasurable experiences.

2. Thou shalt LIE to thy parents about thy sexual experiences, or at best, thou shalt NOT SPEAK OF THEM out of fear and shame.
3. Thou shalt feel GUILTY because of thy falsehoods.

I don't want to live like this anymore, with unnecessary life-squelching emotions, fear, guilt and shame, all associated with sex and love. Sex plus love is the BEST combination, the divine duo. Sex plus love equals ecstasy, and yet in the teen's world, sex plus love equals shame, lies and guilt! No wonder our teens are confused.

What a terrible commandment to give them just as the flower is opening: "Thou shalt not speak of thy ecstasy and joy, thou shalt pretend not to have experienced sex, thou shalt try very hard not to know ecstasy in thy blooming flower of a body, because if you do, thou shalt be DAMNED."

For teens the partner of sex is shame. It ought to be joy! Is joy damned too? Dammed, I'd say, by guilt.

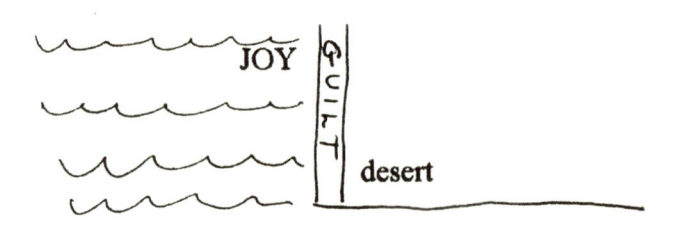

Aside from fear of STDs, what is wrong with free expression of joyous, loving sexuality? Why are we poisoning our teenagers with shame? Is it to keep them from knowing ecstasy? Is it to make them 'work hard' (sublimate their sexual energy into productive energy)?

The teen years are a phase-specific time for initiation into adulthood. Human beings are programmed to be initiated into ecstasy as a rite of passage into adulthood. When a culture misses its cue and does not provide appropriately guided initiation its teens turn to self-initiation. Understanding intuitively that initiation involves danger and breaking with childhood, they try dangerous adult activities such as fast driving, alcohol and drugs, crime, gangs and promiscuous sex. The ones who live through it usually outgrow it, but meanwhile the culture has lost both an opportunity to reinforce its own values as well as the vitalizing creative energy of its teens who use their considerable energy instead to *disrupt* the culture that has neglected to initiate them. The spiritual opening that frequently occurs during adolescence (as during every life transition) is often similarly lost.

We need to rewrite the book on teenage sex. What if guilt was only associated with sex without love? What if 'responsible sex' meant loving yourself and your partner enough not to create a child you're not ready to raise? Enough not to transmit disease? Enough not to cause emotional violence to each other? What if responsible sex meant being responsible for giving joy to your partner? Is love a priority in sex? Why? Why not? 'Love and joy come to you' has been changed to 'shame and death.' We need to change it back.

Men and Women

About Peter and Me

When Peter and I came together in 1987 there was a way that we represented the best of our respective genders. Peter's strength was his mind: brilliant, broad, well-balanced, self-motivated, well-schooled. I sensed the breadth and depth of it and was somewhat in awe. He also had spiritual depth developed during ten years living in Zen Buddhist monasteries in Japan and the US.

My strength was a good understanding of my emotional body and some skill at relationship. Thanks to my maternal ancestors I was a good mother, I understood emotional need and how to meet it in myself, my children and others. I felt grounded in the earth by fifteen years of homesteading in Vermont. I had recently tasted the explosive power of the combination of sexuality and spirituality in an intense affair that turned my inner world upside down and spelled the end of my seventeen-year marriage. Peter, relentlessly moving in the direction of his goal of 'completeness', was now ready for relationship. And sex. Lots of sex! Up front about it when we met at a dance workshop, I naively asked him if he'd mind having a 3-day affair exploring the merging of sex and spirituality. He replied that the dimension of time disappears when entering into an alchemy such as I was proposing. Sex has always been a strong force in our relationship, acting as best-quality glue during our many stormy periods. We figure the three-day affair lasted about three years and then we got down to business.

During the first years of our relationship another alchemy was occurring: an exchange of knowledge male to female and female to male. Peter taught me about world history, philosophy, anthropology, world mythology and science of East and West. He said I was a 'thirsty sponge' absorbing the essence of his twenty years of study. I remember many mornings after delicious nights of love when Peter would tell me what he knew. Our bed was and is our sharing place for intimacies of all kinds. It is in the bed that we make love, it was in the bed that Peter

84

shared his intellectual world with me, and it is in the bed that we together have spent long hours uncovering the path to emotional truth, my gift to Peter. For when you discover emotional truth you have discovered the bedrock upon which you can build a trusting relationship. Without emotional truth, relationship is a sham, play-acting between characters trying to hide from each other and themselves.

So it seems that Peter's oversoul chose me so that he could learn to know his own intimate emotions and could then begin to be in true relationship with himself and the world. My oversoul chose Peter because of his depth and dedication to discovering himself and because my intellect was starving for a bigger picture. To complete our respective pictures, he needed a close-up and I a panorama. We both needed love and wanted sex. We got both and more.

We had a sense from the beginning that something about our coming together was to better understand maleness and femaleness through a deep, eyes-open meeting with Other. He, a solitary intellectual, a serious spiritual seeker and virgin until his mid-thirties. Me, an Earth Mother with two children, newly matriculated into my own deep body-knowing, initiated by the Dark Goddess into the women's way of knowing from the inside out.

Opposite Sides of the Same Coin: The Symbolism of Male and Female Genitalia

> *"The imagery of the human body is really the founding imagery of myth."*
>
> *- Joseph Campbell*

What makes a man a man is that his genitals, his organs for procreation, are on the **outside** of his body. When they are aroused in pleasure his penis fills with blood, stiffens and **points upward** like an arrow, with a linear orientation. Seminal fluid is ejaculated **up** and **out**, with **force**. A man's genitals **stand alone** and apart from the rest of his body, and are **hard** when pleasurably engaged. They are usually **dry** to the touch. They often seem to have a mind of their own, going erect and flaccid at times when their owner would rather they did not. These change are **visible** and **well-defined**.

<u>**Male genitalia:**</u>

outside the body

linear, in the shape of an 'I' or a '1'

direction of fluids: shooting up and out

pointing upward when procreating

alone and apart

semi-independent

visible

dry to the touch

his fluids are always the same

hard when active

What makes a woman a woman is that her organs of procreation are almost entirely on the **inside** of her body. They are hidden in secret dark places never seen by the light of day. They are **moist** all the time. Their secretions, which **change** with her monthly cycle, always **drip downward**. Likewise, babies, her ultimate creative product, emerge by the downward path. There is **no sense of urgency** motivating the release of her reproductive fluids. No matter her weight, size or shape, a woman's genitals are always **soft**, conforming to the shape of their occupant, be it man or babe.

<u>**Female genitalia:**</u>

inside the body

shape of an 'O' or portal

direction of fluids: dripping down

baby emerges downward

not separate from her other organs

predictable cycles affecting her whole body

not visible on the outside

moist

fluids change color and consistency

soft

    The effects of secondary sexual characteristics such as facial hair, breasts, body shape, fat-to-muscle ratio, etc. have been discussed *ad nauseum* by scientists, anthropologists, talk-show hosts and every teenager the world over. Although we identify ourselves and others primarily by gender, rarely is it speculated what the effects might be on our symbol-sensitive psyches of our primary sexual characteristics, our genitals themselves.

    Painting with broad strokes, a man's orientation, like his genitals, is naturally outward. He is concerned mostly with achievement in the outside world represented by his work. His first tools took outward trajectories: spears, knives and arrows that penetrated into the body of the prey. Explorers and builders in their own image, men created space ships, rockets and guns of all kinds that blast off ecstatically outward and upward. Men have built countless skyscrapers shaped like you-know-what. Soaring white church spires pierce the skies of New England, built by proud founding fathers to indicate their sacred orientation.

    It is no surprise, then, that in an era dominated by masculine thinking the divinity should be a singular male who lives in the sky. The masculine sacred ideal, like his male followers' private parts, is clean, dry, up, ecstatic and male. He is not subject to influence by women. The spiritually male world has a linear orientation: hell is down, heaven is up. You are born, live, die and go to heaven or hell. Once it's done, it's done. On the other hand, the story of the dying and resurrecting god (Dionysus, Horus, Jesus) is suspiciously like the life of the penis.

In an ecstatic burst of energy, it ejaculates its precious seed, plays dead for awhile and then is capable of miraculous 'res-erection' amidst amazement and celebration. Of course in the pre-Christian version, death and rebirth of the young son-god happened every year. In the Christian version Jesus dies but does not return to the earth mother to be recycled, rising instead to be with his father until the second coming at the end of the world.

Let's look at women: speaking in generalities and with a 100,000-year perspective, women were mostly concerned with home. Home, children, family, garden. Women were not explorers or hunters. When women invented things it was to better the home environment: agriculture, writing, cooking, pottery. Women kept the circle whole, working primarily inside of it to nurture and bind its inhabitants together. Women are probably responsible for language, as expression of the mother-child breast-bond of love and appreciation. Women's role was to bind her family together. Her specialty was relationship. Her primary relationship was to her infants whom she carried inside her body under her heart for nine months and them nourished from her own breasts until they could walk, talk, run and feed themselves. To secure the lives of her children, proto-human hominid mothers became sexually available at all times. The promise of frequent sex kept the males from straying too far from home, leaving the young vulnerable to attack from large cats and other terrible predators in the night. Tasty morsels.

Is it any wonder that for women, relationship has intrinsic value? Women in general are better at relationship than men because they are built to carry another person inside their bodies. They are biologically programmed to love this infant and to create the best environment for its growth. Men traditionally have had much less concern than women for family relatedness. In high school I learned this saying: "Boys give love to get sex. Girls give sex to get love." Although there are lots of personal variations and exceptions, I suspect that little chestnut has rung more or less true for 500,000 years at least.

For one half million years, men's chief orientation has been exploration *outside* of the home environment. Men have found creative expression in hunting, exploring, building, philosophizing, waging war and finding out about the world through science, engineering and trade. A list of perennial male values might read like this: exploration, adventure, challenge, definition, individuation, all ways in which men can see the mark of their will upon the world.

For one half million years, women's focus like her genitals has been *inside*, on home and family. Her principal creations have happened in the mysterious darkness inside of her own body, creations which are not of the mind, and which have often taken place *in spite of* her will. To keep her children alive she has developed the art of lovemaking and comfort-making and family-making, the fine art of relationship. Love is a gift from the heart of woman.

Throughout human history we've given differing values to the male/outside and female/inside explorations. Briefly summarized, in the Paleolithic period, the age of the cave paintings of France and Spain, men's and women's ways were equally valued. In the Neolithic, the age of agriculture, women's values were emphasized, and in the Patriarchal, men's.

In the 20th century women awakened to the inferiority of being female in a Patriarchal culture. Their first response was to aspire to equal men in areas of masculine achievement, striving to equal and excel at academics, medicine, business, law, politics. We were trying to make them respect us by showing them we could be just as good at being men as they were. In the process we sacrificed our own fundamental feminine values of wholeness, nurturing and the sacred interrelatedness of all things.

In the 21st century we are seeing a rediscovery of feminine values as we experience the many downsides of the masculine-valued world: poverty, greed, ecological destruction, splintered families, splintered psyches. Feminine values are re-emerging at the moment in history when most women in the West have been freed by birth control from the restraints of fulltime childbearing and have had their intellectual capacities sharpened by nearly a century of equal educational opportunity. Feminine values are re-emerging at the moment in history when the world is beginning to have second thoughts about the effects of the unmoderated masculine upon our planetary culture.

Many men, sensing perhaps the poverty of their role as conquerors or industrial cogs are beginning to look more to home, family and child-rearing for personal satisfaction. All of us are beginning to give increased value to our beautiful blue-green home, the Earth, and to feel her distress as our own, responding to her as to one we are *related to* and therefore naturally care about and must care for. The values of relatedness and love begin to re-emerge on a planetary level as the threat to the ecosystem increases.

It is a cliffhanger. Will humans pull out of the Patriarchal greed/alienation dream and begin to reinstate the values of relatedness in time to avert collapse of the ecosystem and death of most animal and plant species, including our own? Stay tuned.

I do not presume to know how we as a planet will get from where we are to where we need to be to survive the next century or two, but I can provide a vision of what it will look like if we successfully pass the test(icles) and matriculate (as in mother-matrix) to the next level of psycho-spiritual development. The men will acknowledge the importance of the primary feminine value of relatedness and its manifestation as love, caring and generosity. Men will have to tether their horses (horsepower) to the hearthstone, acknowledging that their creative exploration and wonderful inventiveness must be harnessed *in service to life,* by closing the energy circle that is now wide open spewing its precious seed to the wind.

Women's task is to re-animate her intellect in harmony with her emotional body-knowing so she can speak her truth from that core place within. Parroting the Patriarchs will not wash in the next age. Women's knowing needs to come from deep inside. Women need to connect with themselves there and then *speak their truth with no hesitation or shame.*

> *Women, you are connected.*
> *Women, you are connected to all life.*
> *Women, your blood flows in the ocean*
>   *green and blue, red and true.*

Women you are the salt of the seven seas.

Women, your bones are the rocks.

The Standing Stones sing

        your

                song.

Women, your two hearts* beat with the rhythm of the tides and its light-dark-light mistress, the moon.

*The moon, the mistress of the dance by whose shining face and changing belly we were led into **our** 'moon', our menses, our human/divine womanness ebbing and flowing alternating dark blood with white milk according to the laws of love and the laws of cyclical womanish spiraling changing*

NATURE who is also a MOTHER.

Nature who is the mother of the life-death-life cycle,

The cycle of light-dark-light

        and then dark

                and then light.

The mothering is in the moving, and in the knowing of the truth of cycles.

The cycles

that guide us and affect us and ARE us and yet now we are called to transcend.

The Father teaches us to transcend the cycles.

The Father is the mind, the head, the spirit, the above.

The Father teaches us to love our amazing minds.

The Mother teaches us to love our amazing bodies.

*The Mother is about **uniting** by surrendering to the endless cycles of nature of which we are part and parcel.*

*The Father is about **separating** by transcending our earthly cycles of suffering and death, to soar above on blissful wings of spirit.*

No, ladies, it is not time to knock down our fathers and enthrone our mothers in their places. It is time to marry our mothers to our fathers, internally, and to know that this is good.

*It is time to know that **we are the blessed miraculous fruits of this holy union***

> *of Timelessness and Time*
>
> *of Heaven and Earth*
>
> *of Wave and Particle.*

Yes.

Women,

DO YOU HEAR ME?

And if you do, can you pass this on to your men?

(*The uterus is about the same size as the heart and is, like the heart, made of smooth muscle tissue.)

Making Love - Winter 1991

"'Now I will tell you the secret of the creation. Sex is the same in men and women; the ultimate moment of ecstasy in sexual relationship is the same in both...It is the sweetest thing on earth; nothing is sweeter than that. And it is given to men for the sake of procreation.'"

~Guruji, a Sufi Master as quoted by Irina Tweedie

Peter and I made love this morning as we often do, an hour or so after awakening. Our room is large and full of light. Our mattress is on a raised platform tucked into one corner of the room, originally built as the music platform. Indeed it is the place where Thunder Heart, our council drum, is played for the Winter Solstice gathering. This room is our reading room, our dancing room, our playroom, our working room, the seed-womb room where most of our creative ideas are hatched, right in the bed where we so often make love. We can always hear the stream outside, we can always see the sky and the dark forest on the opposite bank of the stream. Birds sometimes visit our feeder. We grow our inner garden here: winter-potted flowers, a rosemary dug up from last year's summer garden, a fragrant sweet olive bush to perfume our days and nights, and a graceful ten-foot-tall avocado tree that followed me from New York City to Vermont as a newlywed over 20 years ago. The garden of our dreaming is tended in this room with eight windows open to the sky and three fat rafters painted peach to resemble ribs protecting the tender heart of our happiness.

Down the narrow spiraling stair into the 'hold' is where the work of everyday living goes on: the boiler room (woodstove), the galley-kitchen, the 'head' we flush with a bucket, and of course the telephone. Downstairs, below decks, is a warren of small dark cozy rooms with the sound and sight of the stream rushing by. But up here on the upper deck we are open to the sky!

The mechanics of our lovemaking is very simple on these mornings. We snuggle closer with gentle greetings. He moves on top of me, my legs entwining his. We become the ocean, ebbing and flowing, moving easily into the depths of the familiar pool we have created in our four years together. Peter almost never ejaculates any more, maybe once a month when I am menstruating. Instead we seem to dive like dolphins inside of one another, becoming one with waves and swells of liquid ecstasy. I am amazed at the similarity of our experiencing of sex. I was describing our lovemaking to a younger friend, a man who had recently fallen in love, with the hope of expanding his horizons. I told him how Peter moves inside me until a threshold of sensation-emotion-energy is reached. Then he stops at the peak, just before orgasm, and we experience something like a mushroom cloud of rising and expanding together. After the mushroom loses a bit of altitude we pump it up again for another rise, and on and on until the flow of desire ebbs. Later Peter read my description, agreeing and affirming our common experiencing of this most delicious phenomenon.

Later I wondered what the correlation might possibly be between my sexual experiences as a teenager, as a young wife for seventeen years and of today, for subjectively they are so very different. Perhaps the common thread is seeking ecstasy *through the body*. There seems to be an intuitive knowing that sex is an avenue to ecstasy. At first it is only a vague indication of direction, like a salmon swimming in the sea and tasting the hint of fresh water. Turning gradually toward the mouth of the river, she heads ever upstream into fresher water and finally into the falls, leaping over rocks and boulders to get to the source. Always she is guided by a bodily knowing of the direction that must be taken to fulfill the promise of this individual life and the life of the species.

What my lifetime's diversity of sexual experiences have in common is swimming in the water. As I get closer to the source my knowing grows keener and more discerning, as the salmon's senses must sharpen to allow her to navigate in shallow rushing water. A sense of being near the goal heightens all the senses, strengthening the urge and affirming the knowing, making it super-conscious. The knowing is this: sexual ecstasy is the same as spiritual ecstasy and I CAN REACH IT THROUGH MY BODY.

It is as though the act of intercourse opens the inner womb of spirit to allow the divine to enter. The willingness to enter into sexual activity is an opening to experiencing in your own body the electrical mystical currents that are at the very heart of God. First in droplets like icicles melting in the sun, then sparking streams and small still pools or occasional springs of clear water for the delight of the thirsty. Gradually the predictable steady volume of wide rivers of joy flows through the body (etheric, astral, dream bodies?) and finally a total immersion in the ocean of undifferentiated ecstasy that is SOURCE, that is the pool of beginning of all being. The ONE.

The MERE, the mother-sea of at-one-ness, the ecstasy of complete belonging, the freedom to breathe and move and be supported by the ALL THAT IS. That is the promise and the origin of the sexual urge that starts us on our journey of the first kiss and sometimes leads down broken pathways of betrayal and violence as well. How many thousands of salmon are caught in nets, foiled by hydro dams, poisoned by factories and sewage, never to reach the spawning grounds?

But the healing promise remains. May it be fulfilled in each of us.

Pleasure-Bonding and Erotiphobia

"For 2,000 years or more man has been subjected to a systematic effort to transform him into an ascetic animal. He remains a pleasure-seeking animal. Parental discipline, religious denunciations of bodily pleasure, and philosophical exaltation of the life of reason have all left man overtly docile, but secretly in his unconscious unconvinced, and therefore neurotic. Man remains unconvinced because in infancy he tasted the fruit of the tree of life, and knows that it is good, and never forgets."
~Norman O. Brown, Life Against Death

"John Salvi III, the tormented loner accused of killing two women in a shooting spree at two Brookline, Mass. Health clinics last week, is at the far lunatic end of a disturbing continuum: a rising tide of resistance to women's rights.

Though Salvi may be a disturbed individual, his action apparently was inspired by a movement that is gaining strength, ***a new Puritanism,*** *that wants to punish women for sexuality and to insist that the only acceptable kind of family is the one in which men rule the roost...dark and dangerous forces are at play I the land, and we disregard them at our peril."*

- Caryl Rivers, The L.A. Times, 1/8/1995

The Puritans founded this country, and their main thing was **erotiphobia**.

Erotiphobia is fear of Eros, fear of breaking down boundaries.

Above all, **erotiphobia** is **fear of deep pleasure.**

Erotiphobia prevents **adult pleasure bonding,**

96

resulting in **hedonism**
and broken families.

Adult pleasure bonding
includes **sex**
and must take place in the context
of a **committed**
long term
relationship.
The **committed long term relationship**
becomes much richer, fuller, safer and more satisfying
if **adult pleasure bonding** is achieved.
One's ability to successfully achieve **adult pleasure bonding**
depends to a large extent
upon one's experience of
mother-infant pleasure bonding
during infancy (a gift passed
from mother
to child)
AND to the degree to which one has internalized
religious messages that pleasure
is sinful, added to advertisers' messages that
pleasure can be divorced from a relational context.
Divorcing pleasure from a relational context
creates **hedonism**
because
the human organism has a basic biological need
to experience pleasure IN THE BODY.
If basic needs are not able to be met by the

conscious mind in healthy ways,

they will be met

by the unconscious mind (acting through the body)

in whatever ways it can.

Hence if denied the natural nurturing experience of pleasure

in the context of loving trusting relationship,

the pleasure-hungry human (we are all pleasure-hungry)

will seek pleasure

where he/she can find it.

Alone or sporadically,

from "things" or by using people as "things"

trying to satisfy a hunger

but not knowing really what food even looks like

or how to cook it

much less grow a garden full.

Pleasure Bonding: two versions

Infant-to-mother pleasure bonding
- a body-to-body experience infused with love
- includes gestation, breast-feeding, gentle caring touch
- mother takes care of infant
- unconditional loving acceptance of infant by mother
- in this atmosphere the infant feels safe to grow physically, emotionally and psychologically
- a long-term relationship involving commitment by the mother to the child
- the child is born trusting

Adult-to-adult pleasure bonding

- same: a body-to-body experience infused with love
- includes hugging, kissing, making love, physical intimacies, caring touch
- physical caretaking is incidental, not primary
- unconditional loving acceptance of adult by adult partner
- in this atmosphere both partners feel safe to grow emotionally and psychologically
- requires a long-term committed relationship because:
- trust takes time to develop in the adult

If the infant's needs for love, caring and intimacy were not met by the mother or were over-done (smothering), it will be difficult for the adult to trust enough to achieve the adult pleasure-bond. But healing is possible if we understand the original blueprint and where our personal story has deviated from it so we can set out to repair the damage.

The Original Blueprint

The original blueprint for the human species sets up a wonderfully intense total-body experience of pleasure before birth (inside the mother's body) and after birth in contact with the mother's body. Love, devotion, merging, pleasure, are all experienced together. As the child grows he moves naturally and gradually away from the merged pleasure of mother toward an understanding of himself as a complete individual inhabiting his own pleasure-filled body. At puberty he begins to explore sexuality and eventually finds a compatible mate. The two together recreate gradually the physical pleasure, intimacy and trust both partners experienced as infants with the mother, with certain crucial differences.

Nature's purpose in creating pleasurable experience is to encourage bonding, strengthen the trusting loving fulfilling bond between individuals, and create more humans. Pleasure feels good. We move toward a person in whose presence we feel pleasure. The experience is repeated. We begin to trust and to love and to offer pleasure, trust and love, subconsciously recalling our original matrix where pleasure, trust and love reinforced our first long-term relationship. Family feeling is born, nurtured by feelings of love, trust and *pleasure.* It is in the context of adult pleasure bonding that new life is created. The child is conceived in the pleasure bond matrix, is gestated and born into it, is able to safely grow into an emotionally healthy adult ready to recreate the matrix with an adult partner, and so on.

infant-mother pleasure bonding → child grows up → adult pleasure bonding → creates babies → (cycle)

Pitfalls

The first obvious pitfall is a failure in the mother-infant pleasure bond. If the mother is unable to feel physical pleasure in relation to her infant (touching, holding, breastfeeding, etc.) then of course the child is going to have trouble experiencing bodily pleasure in a healthy context at every stage of life.

But assuming the mother-infant pleasure bond was for the most part successful, what are some factors that could interfere with the adult's ability to experience successful pleasure bonding?

1. Feelings of shame and guilt associated with sex and body caused by sexual abuse of the child
2. Feelings of shame and guilt associated with sex and body caused by religious teachings, including sexual mutilation of males and females in the name of religion

3. Feelings of inferiority associated with one's body caused by media/advertising messaging that idealizes one rare body type at the expense of the majority who do not fit the ideal
4. Confusion caused by media/advertising messages that tell us our hunger for pleasurable experience can be satisfied by *things* (cigarettes, jeans, cars, beer, chocolate)

When Nature's pleasure bonding cycle is broken by messages of guilt and shame we are unable to feel good about our bodies and are unable to experience pleasure without guilt.

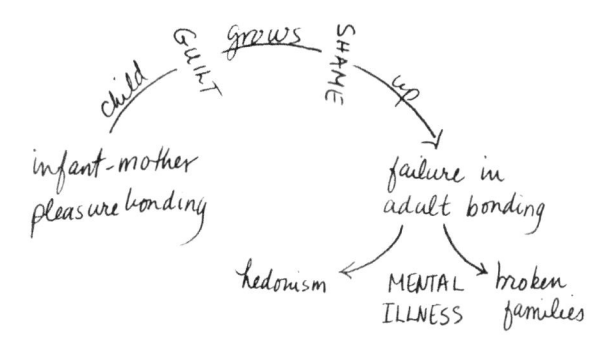

[Diagram: a cycle showing infant-mother pleasure bonding → child → GUILT → grows → SHAME → up → failure in adult bonding → broken families / MENTAL ILLNESS → hedonism]

Pleasurable experiences with *things* are always going to be a poor substitute for the real thing. Nature intended that pleasure be experienced in the context of a loving trusting committed relationship to other human beings. The image of an infant in an incubator or 'isolette' as they used to be called, keeps appearing to me. When the newborn's needs are thwarted or when she feels pain, rage happens.

> *RAGE whose redness swells the veins of eye and face*
> *eyelids and fists shut like tiny vises*
> *against outrageous treatment*
> *by gargantuan strangers*
> *who DO NOT SEE ME*

In the early 21st century we are seeing a lot more rage in adults than previously. We also see an awful lot of depression, guilt and anxiety that are probably covering repressed rage caused by basic human needs going unmet.

> *"Every one of us is so afraid to become aware of our real needs. Becoming aware of our real needs hurts so terribly because deep inside we know how starved we are. We cannot believe this lack can ever be filled...We feel a terrific, tremendous anger that our needs cannot be met...Our rage is caused by our frustration at what we cannot realize in our lives: the need for growing, maturing and becoming adult."*
>
> ~Walter Lechler, M.D.

Healing Suggestions for people who have trouble with pleasure

- Swimming (emphasis on whole body sensations, relaxation, enjoyment)
- Dancing (any kind that makes you feel happy)
- Authentic Movement
- Giving and receiving nourishing massage
- Masturbation as a sacrament of self love
- Making love as a conscious sacred ritual
- Investigating your beliefs, such as "I don't deserve to have pleasure", "pleasure is not for me" etc. using self-enquiry such as The Work of Byron Katie
- Movement therapy or other body-centered psychotherapy

Adult Relationships

The path toward successful and satisfying adult pleasure bonding will be much less fraught with danger if both the goals and the pitfalls are clearly marked at the outset of the journey.

Cultural erotiphobia often prevents individuals from exploring the rich territory of the adult pleasure bond.

Co-dependency

If adult pleasure bonding is attempted before differentiation from the parents is complete it becomes substitution, where both partners are seeking a mother's or father's perfect nurturance for their incomplete inner child. Co-dependent relationships result when both partners are seeking to be fulfilled by the other.

When both partners are relatively emotionally mature they can meet as non-dependent equals and the pleasure bond can deepen and ripen in all spheres: physical, emotional and spiritual. Emotions are often the most immature component of a personality because emotional wholeness is neither taught nor understood in our culture. Both partners must fully explore and mature their *emotional* natures before they can stand face to face with each other as equals instead of projecting 'safety' or 'bitch/bastard' (the two most common mommy/daddy projections) onto the mate. (For excellent treatment of this subject, see works by Harville Hendrix in recommended reading).

Challenges for Conscious Couples

Learning adult emotional intimacy presents different challenges for men and women. In general emotional intimacy is relatively easy for women because they are biologically wired to be intimately related to their infants, and this wiring generalizes to others whom they love. For the unscarred woman, emotional intimacy is second nature. For most men emotional bonding requires a double sacrifice.

First a man must curtail the (unconscious) masculine biological imperative to spread his seed far and wide to as many wombs as possible in hopes that his genetic heritage will be passed on. Instead he must seek the Holy Grail in the heart of ONE woman, or at least one woman at a time.

Second, he must surrender his isolation, becoming as a supplicant at the Altar of Woman, where he can learn intimacy, nurturing and love.

The man must see his double sacrifice as both necessary and advantageous in his quest for a fulfilled life. Otherwise he may not be persuaded to relinquish these two important aspects of his masculine nature. It helps if he remembers that sacrifice, discipline and denial of natural urgings always play an essential role in the masculine spiritual journey.

The epidemic of men unable to commit to lasting relationship is based in part on the man's legitimate fear of being emotionally smothered by the woman if he relinquishes his emotional isolation. Woman's challenge is to merge *appropriately* with her mate by refraining from infantilizing him with a too large dose of instinctual mothering. Too much mothering most often manifests as taking care of him or wanting him to be a certain way.

In summary, the man must surrender emotionally to the woman, letting down his fortress walls in order to learn to merge with her in love, while the woman must learn to separate her talent for emotional intimacy from her need to mother, control or manipulate her partner IN ANY WAY. These are not easy lessons for either partner, I assure you, and can take a bit of trial and error on the part of both.

Fortunately for us all it is not necessary to be totally emotionally mature before entering into adult pleasure bonding (whew!). Committed relationship can be seen as the finishing fire in which one's immaturities rise to the surface to be experienced, explored and released on the sacrificial Altar of Love. Both partners act as second matrix for each other as they grow together in emotional maturity. Strangely, it is not *co*dependence but emotional *in*dependence that is the result of intimate *conscious* co-exploration of vulnerability. If the process were more generally understood, more couples would be able to use relationship to further their personal growth toward wholeness, seeing conscious relationship as a nurturing spiritual and emotional home base where both partners' needs can be met, including and especially their need to safely grow into themselves in an atmosphere of loving acceptance.

Chapter Seven

Women, Religion and Lies

Dialogue from a Calvin and Hobbes cartoon by Bill Waterson:

Calvin: Do you hate being a girl?

Suzie: It's gotta be better than the alternative.

Calvin: What's it like? Is it like being a bug?

Suzie: Like a **WHAT?!**

Calvin: I imagine bugs and girls have a dim perception that nature played a cruel trick on them, but they lack the intelligence to really comprehend the magnitude of it.

(Next frame shows Calvin upside down in front of his locker, seeing stars)

Calvin: I must've put my finger on it.

Why Women Have Trouble with Patriarchal Religions

> *"Is that a dagger or a crucifix I see*
> *you hold so tightly in your hand?"*
>
> -lyric from a song by Peter Gabriel

Religions of the Book

The Christian religion is based upon the Bible, a collection of books written, edited and re-edited by males. Judaism is based on the Torah and Talmud, collections of books written and until recently studied exclusively by males. The teachings of Islam were recorded by males in their sacred book, the Koran. All three of these religions were born in the same desert, a tiny corner of the globe, to a people to whom the Earth (the sacred Mother) was not hospitable.

From nomadic people came three nomadic religions that were carried, along with their sacred texts, around the world, thriving in spite of many transplantings. It was Joseph Campbell who coined the phrase 'religions of the book' to describe Judaism, Christianity and Islam.

We might ask ourselves why other religions have not similarly spread across our globe?

It is because Hindu, Shinto and Native American, Inuit, Zulu and hundreds more are connected with local 'spirits of place' and cannot be transplanted to another place. Balinese gods are *in and of* the live volcano Gunung Agung that lies at the center of their beautiful little island. The Goddess Nyi Loro Kidul is *in and of* the blue-green Java Sea. The divine imagination of the people cannot be separated out from the sacred land that gave it birth. Sacred mountains such as the Black Hills or Mount Fuji stubbornly refuse to be moved to another continent. In short, **religions whose sacred elements are connected to or dwell within the Earth (the Mother's body) are not portable.** In Earth-based religions, Nature is understood to be alive, mostly benevolent, and powerful. Forces of both good and evil are recognized as divine. In Earth-based religions the human role is that of mediator, observer, propitiator, appreciator and balancer of natural divine forces through prayer, celebration, ritual, fasting, etc.

'Religions of the book,' on the other hand, have historically viewed Nature as inanimate and generally inhospitable, as something to be tamed by man with the help of his one single celibate male God who is outside His creation. All three of these religions have traditionally viewed women as spiritually inferior to men, as evidenced by all-male gods, all-male prophets and traditionally all-male priesthoods.

Women: An essential difference

Because of the dominant nature of the sex drive in men it is necessary and appropriate for men to subdue their natural sexual urges in order to come into balance with themselves and the universal principle of harmony. If this were not true there would not be the ideal of celibacy for men at some stage in their lives that we see expressed in nearly every major religion.

It is true that most spiritual practices advocated by male-centered religions are inappropriate for women. It is appropriate that women not be Christian priests or monks, Catholic popes or Muslim ayatollahs, Buddhist Roshis or Indian Sadhus. It is appropriate that women not be ascetics of any kind.

For men, the spiritual path involves curtailment of masculine excesses, often involving physical pain and suffering. Examples are the Native American practice of sweat lodge (enduring extreme heat while sitting naked and crowded on the dirt floor of a suffocating dark smoky enclosure) and Sundance (the dancer achieves altered states of consciousness by piercing his chest and attaching himself by his skin to a cord tied to a pole, around which he dances in the heat of the summer solstice, for three days). Medieval Christian monks wore hair shirts under their robes so they would not get too comfortable on this Earth. In Zen meditation one sits cross-legged for hours in pursuit of mindfulness, sometimes causing excruciating pain the spine and legs of the novice. Serious followers of the monastic life shave their heads and take vows of celibacy. All of these practices and many more were intended originally only for men.

If the spiritual path for men involves discipline and denial of the body, women's practices require surrender and a willingness to follow the natural rhythms of the body. Women do not require additional ritualized pain and suffering such as sweat lodge, because in the course of their lives, Nature gives them ample pain and suffering. A man and a woman may both enjoy making love, but we all know it is the woman who bears the consequences of that act, be it pregnancy, abortion, miscarriage, labor and childbirth, death in childbed or birth of an infant for whom she must care.

Life of Woman

Consider some common events in the life of most women: menstruation, lovemaking, marriage, pregnancy, childbirth, child rearing, nursing the sick, attending the dying.

Throughout she is creating the loving fabric of family, finding ways to weave her family members closer to each other in harmonious relationship. Women's natural imperative is relationship, relating the parts to the whole and filling the whole with love. Thus if a woman surrenders herself to this 'natural' role, she will experience in her lifetime a great deal of pain and suffering, both physical and emotional. Ask any mother if she does not agree that *loving*, the simple and natural act of loving the people in her family, does not at times cause her intense suffering. Hence she does not need to create for herself trials by fire or by any other means. She simply must surrender to the full experience of living and loving as they manifest in her life through her body and heart.

Yet if a woman surrenders to her biological role without spiritual or personal awareness she remains asleep in her instinctual functioning. A woman's challenge is to awaken her powers of mind so she can articulate and value her experience, contributing important insight as to the nature of the universe – insights about relatedness that men may not have access to except through the eyes and experience of women.

Confusion and resentment arise in women because all of our major religions are modeled on the male's requirements for spiritual advancement. Many of our religions teach that the body is inferior, that women are spiritually inferior, when the truth is that women are not inferior, they are different. Women feel lost, unloved and unseen by Patriarchal religions because women are invisible to religious traditions with Patriarchal tunnel vision. Patriarchal religions are wearing blinders looking single-pointedly UP toward heaven, enlightenment, nirvana, etc. They cannot see that women need a very different but equally valid set of practices.

What women seek and crave is religious and spiritual principles and practices that reflect their knowing, their particular type of awareness and their biologically based experience of the world. Women need a religion acknowledging cycles, birth death and rebirth, and the connectedness between all things.

> *we need a god who bleeds now...*
>
> *spreads her lunar vulva & showers us in shades of scarlet*
>
> *thick & warm like the breath of her*
>
> *our mothers tearing to let us in*
>
> *...i am not wounded i am bleeding to life*
>
> *we need a god who bleeds now*
>
> *whose wounds are not the end of anything*
>
> — *from a poem by Ntozake Shange*

Women have not found affirmation of their experience in traditional manifestations of the major Patriarchal religions. If we are to find examples of religions that incorporate feminine experience and values, we must leave for a moment the portable 'religions of the book' and seek guidance from localized Earth-centered traditions such as Native American women's practices, Shinto in Japan, and Pagan Europe. Since these are not portable but have sprung up 'in situ' from the Earth herself and are manifestations of Earth's energies at a particular location, we must not attempt to recreate whole cloth the tradition of another people and place. We can study them to find what is true and then model our own rituals on theirs, recognizing that we are creating a new and different set of rituals arising out of our needs as modern people living in a particular bioregion.

Because women are innately connected to Earth, women (and men in traditional indigenous cultures) naturally resonate with roundness, solidity, cycles of nature, interconnectedness, the dark, and bodily experience. Religions embodying feminine experience emphasize inclusion instead of separateness, another masculine value. For example, Hindu has many gods and goddesses, all manifestations of the One. Feminine experience dictates that ALL experience is divine, just as all of her children are lovable. No child is excluded from the Mother's breast for unacceptable behavior, whereas 'sinful' Christians are sent to burn forever in Hell. At play here are the masculine principles of separation and punishment, versus the feminine principles of inclusion and forgiveness. Of course excesses are possible on both sides. I am not advocating a total rejection of the values of separation and self-definition, but recognition that the feminine experience is different and equally valuable. Inclusion of feminine experience is needed to rebalance our world and stop the lemming race toward the cliff edge that the Patriarchal period has initiated.

Women's experience is different. Women's experience is valid. Women's experience is valuable and necessary if we are to survive. This applies to women's spiritual experience as well as to her biological experience.

It would be helpful if religious leaders of today would acknowledge that their traditions have been based on the masculine path. It would be good to begin to manifest an equal feminine path for their female adherents, with equal recognition of the feminine as divine. In any case, the feminine aspects of God must be recognized as **no less than half** of the Godhead. There is no reason why existing religions can't modify their approach to reflect growth in understanding of the feminine face and body of god. In this age of gender bending, if masculine and feminine pathways were created and articulated, people of both genders could choose which path suits them best, or create their own mix of practices.

What do feminine spiritual practices look like? For a start, they tend to happen in circles. There is, I am told, a Native American practice called Women's Council where women come together in a circle to listen to each other and to give council. Men do this, too. There is a wonderful description of Navaho men wrapped in their blankets, sitting in silence all night, listening for the truth to arise, in the wonderful novel <u>The Man Who Killed the Deer</u> by Frank Waters. In a hybrid ceremony called Journey to the Grandmothers, women gather to go within seeking wisdom from one of eight spiritual 'grandmothers' (Grandmother Sun, Grandmother Death, Grandmother Midwife, etc.) to obtain answers to their own or others' questions. Using this simple ritual, even 'ordinary' women are able to tap into wisdom beyond their personal experience. It is a direct line that requires no hierarchy, where everyone is respected as a channel of the divine.

Women's religious practices would sanctify the natural cycles of a woman's life: menarche, marriage, childbirth, menopause. There is a wonderful Navajo ceremony for girls at menarche, where the whole community gathers to celebrate her entry into womanhood. Croning is a Pagan ceremony for a woman entering menopause, a time when a woman's 'wise blood' begins to be retained inside of her body. Croning recognizes and honors the wisdom of older women, seeing it as a resource for the community. It goes without saying that childbirth is a sacred transformative creative event and would be recognized as sacrament.

Dancing, especially in circles, is included in sacred ritual in nearly all Native cultures. "In every culture where the goddess is revered, women dance in ecstatic celebration of the sacred energy that can be felt and enjoyed in the body..."(Vicki Noble).

Dance expresses emotion through the body. Dancing in circles expresses communion with cycles of moon and sun, tides and seasons, as well as being an expression of community. A sense of physical and spiritual union with divine energies can easily be reached through simple repetitive group folk dance, provided it is done with sacred intention. Dancing in a circle says "we are equal parts of the moving wholeness" and "we are all Divine". And it is fun. You can feel the pleasure of dancing while you are praying!

And while we're on the subject of religion, how about having a religion that sanctifies pleasure, enjoyment and beauty? I am struck by this line in the Charge of the Goddess by Doreen Valiente as translated by Starhawk: **"All acts of love and pleasure are my ritual."** How unlike any of our familiar religions. Love and pleasure. *All acts of love and pleasure are my ritual.* Well, why not?

The Jesus Thing

"Do you connect with Jesus?" a friend asked me in the mid-1990s. I said "No, not any more." Raised in a devout Episcopalian family, I used to connect with Jesus, but not any more. Perhaps I've thrown the baby out with the bathwater, I can't say for sure, but when I started to understand the depth to which I had been lied to by 'the Church', I could no longer feel the old magic. It wasn't that I was angry with Jesus. I was angry at God himself, and at the Church Fathers. To my eyes, Jesus' message had been manipulated to such an extent that I could not feel the true shape of it. Some of it certainly is authentic enlightened teaching, and I believe the man did exist, but the bible. I just can't get into the bible.

Do you know about the Council of Nicaea? In the fourth century A.D., Christians began to have some political power, so they decided to close ranks. In 325 A.D. at Nicaea a group of organization-hungry bishops decided which of the many writings about Jesus suited their purposes, declared their choices to be the only true versions of the story, and *Voila!* We have the Four Gospels. In the process they destroyed the losing versions, cleaned up any 'unclear' passages (read: things they did not understand or disapproved of) and toned down the importance of female followers, especially Mary Magdalene who some say was Jesus' constant companion and most-loved disciple.

Constantine, the first Christian emperor, murdered his wife and son because he suspected she was unfaithful. And this was only the beginning. The coming of Christianity meant license to slaughter heathens and wantonly destroy centuries of accumulated knowledge from the pre-Christian world.

> "...the church proceeded methodically to ...suppress all information that did not emanate from the church itself. They first closed down the ancient Greek academies and then set about burning the books of the great classical poets, philosophers, and scholars, setting knowledge back fifteen hundred years and necessitating the painful *rediscovery* in modern times of truths and facts well known even to the early Greek sages. In the fifth century

they turned their...attention to the great library at Alexandria, the last repository of the wisdom and knowledge of the ancients. They burned the books and razed the buildings and carried off to Constantinople whatever they thought might be of monetary value."
~Elizabeth Gould Davis

Beautiful temples and statuary in Greek cities and throughout the countryside were destroyed or converted to Christian reliquaries, with pieces of the bodies of Christian saints sold for profit.

No wonder they call it the Dark Ages. The Christian world *created* the Dark Ages. I'd been taught that it was the heroic but humble Christian monks who preserved learning in monasteries during the Dark Ages, as heathens ravaged Europe. There is no doubt a piece of truth in that version, but one must realize that it was in the name of Christ that much of European and Middle Eastern learning and culture was destroyed. Sunday school and public school left out that part, as they did any mention of the Burning Times, a three-hundred year wave of church-sanctioned persecution, torture and execution of multitudes of European women and men for practicing the old Earth-based indigenous religion.

At one time Europeans must have had a deeply sacred connection to the land as do remaining indigenous peoples around the globe. Apparently and tragically it was Christianity that uprooted the European indigenous religions and culture. I have grieved the loss of the European earth-connection, my own ancestry being mainly French, German and English, but I am able to take solace in the fact that it took hundreds of years of relentless persecution, political murder and torture to wipe out the European earth-spirit bond, attesting to the depth of the beliefs and the tenacity of the people who held them. It is hypothesized that the dramatic success of the Black Plague during the Middle Ages was at least in part a result of the demise of thousands of healers, sourcerers and herbalists put to death in the name of the Christian faith. Without their knowledge of herbs and healing, the black plague was able to spread unopposed, taking with it the lives of over one-third the population of Europe.

The way I see it now, Christianity was basically a political movement with a portable religion conveniently attached, a religion that could be used to mold the conquered populace to the will of the conquerors. Where is the message of Jesus Christ in all this? I have no idea, and that's the essence of the problem. It might be that Jesus' true message was so radical and anti-establishment that it spawned a new rigidity in an attempt to contain the message.

One way to view Church history is to see the Church hierarchy playing the role of the Old Testament god, Yaweh, making rules, passing judgment and generally being all-powerful. The masses of Christian believers were given the role of Yaweh's meek and mild son, Jesus. The followers were told to be penitent, humble, self-effacing and forgiving, to be child-like in their innocence, their willingness to follow blindly and in their deference to the authority of the parental church. Good Christians like good children were not even supposed to think about sex, much less enjoy it or perform it unless married, and preferably for purposes of procreation only. I wonder if this isn't because sex is an *adult* activity and Christians were supposed to think always of themselves as *children* of God. "Thou shalt not commit *adult*ery." Is that what Jesus the enlightened teacher had in mind? I doubt it.

So how can we tell who Jesus is or was? To me the mythical Jesus is a somewhat sad character whose powerful revolutionary mystical message of love was co-opted and obscured by two thousand years of self-serving politicians calling themselves Christian. This is still happening today. The followers, like so many sheep have tried to make the best of being *good* sheep and have been dutifully fleeced, sheared, castrated and sacrificed. And how can Jesus be the Lamb of God and the Good Shepherd at the same time? I guess I just don't get it.

The only way Jesus works for me is Ayla's way, to see him as half the Christ with Mary Magdalene as the other half. Research into the Gnostic Gospels and other early source material lends credence to this story. It is odd that Jesus is supposed to have been an unmarried rabbi in a culture where it was expected that a rabbi would be the head of his own family.

What would it take for me to get behind Jesus, to be able to accept him as my teacher, someone to emulate? I would like a Jesus who was in right relationship with women. This means he would be a fully sexual male, preferably engaged in a healthy co-equal partnership with an equally wise and enlightened fully human fully divine fully sexual flesh and blood woman. If not the 'full partnership' model, at least give me a Jesus who loves and respects women and says so in his teaching, like Pope Francis or the 14th Dalai Lama do. This kind of Jesus I could get behind.

I don't know if rumors of Jesus' sexuality have been around for centuries or if this stuff is new, but I do find it interesting that the possibility of a sexual Jesus is being explored in the arts. In the film The Last Temptation of Christ and in the bestselling book The DaVinci Code we are given a Jesus who was lover to Mary Magdalene and may have fathered a child by her. If we could raise Mary Magdalene from harlot to goddess, Jesus' partner in body and spirit, now that would be a Second Coming I could get excited about.

The following was performed on stage by the author in Brattleboro, Vermont, on Feb 23, 1992, in conjunction with "Heartwork: Art Emerging from Silence", a multimedia exhibition of art and performance by survivors of sexual abuse and intimate violence.

Spiritual Sexual Abuse

I have a confession to make. I have not experienced physical sexual abuse in this lifetime. I was not afraid in the night. I did not have my innocence ripped away like the sheet off a bed. I did not live in fear of heavy footsteps coming down the hall, as did several of my friends who were abused by their fathers, step-fathers and uncles. I have not been raped nor molested. I have never even had an abusive lover.

The abuse I am recovering from takes a much subtler form. It is the pervasive, continual devaluing of the soul, the self at the center, the delicate inborn sensing mechanism that we may call 'the feminine.' To me it is the She, the One Who Knows.

My name for this kind of abuse is Spiritual Sexual Abuse. I believe that virtually everyone who lives in the parts of the world that are heavily influenced by patriarchal religions experiences this kind of subtle abuse daily.

At the heart of each of the three 'religions of the book' (Christian, Jewish, Islam) and to a lesser extent in patriarchal eastern religions as well, are

>FEAR of sexuality

>HATRED of the feminine, and

>LOATHING of the self.

It is this matrix of fear, loathing and hatred that makes possible many of the crippling acts of physical and emotional violence so common in our world today.

Because emotional climate and behaviors are passed on to us through our mothers and their mothers and so on back through the generations, every man, woman and child of

Western European descent is a SURVIVOR of the legacy of the witch burnings. Hundreds of thousands or more* of Western Europeans (80% of them women) were tortured and killed

> for being healers
>
> for being sexually attractive
>
> for singing or showing exuberance
>
> for owning property
>
> for aiding women in childbirth
>
> for dancing in the forest
>
> for practicing their indigenous religion
>
> for speaking truth.

I hated the Puritans for their severity until I realized they were SURVIVORS. Denial and scapegoating must have become a way of life for most Western Europeans in order to survive the horrific centuries of Church-inflicted violence against women and practitioners of indigenous religion, enacted for motives of power and greed.

This is the legacy Europeans brought to the New World, a legacy we are still passing on to our children.

(*estimates run from 100,000 to eight million)

In Love with the Father God

'When I was a little girl,
when I was a little girl...'
   ~ lyric by Paul Simon

When I was a little girl, Daddy was a god. Mommy was a goddess. This is the way it always is.

Mommy and Daddy took me, their adored first child, to church. St. Giles Episcopal Church. I loved it there. They had candles. It was dark and mysterious, with strange wonderful smells and dark carved wooden benches. There was singing. I loved it.

A tiny girl barely able to walk, Daddy carried me into the church. I saw the candles at the altar. "Birthday party!" I crowed, thrilled with the whole thing. My father proudly told anyone who would listen, of my uncensored reaction to seeing a bishop for the first time: "Look at the funny man! Look at the funny man!"

I got the message very young that God was in the church, but it was not a Mommy God. The mommies sat in the pews wearing their hats and veils and red lipstick. Some of the daddies dressed up funny and went up by the birthday candles, at the front where everybody was looking. There was a carving of a man up there on the wall, a sad man with no clothes on.

I think that must have been the beginning of my love affair with the Father God. I loved His church, everything about it. I was a girl, so I guess I knew I could never go up there and do the important stuff at the altar. But there was no reason I couldn't love the men who were up there, like my Daddy. I was so proud of him!

I guess I was a pragmatist. I didn't spend any time wondering where the Mommy God was, just greedily taking what was offered. Maybe I was a spiritual junkie, I don't know, but I do remember the feeling of falling in love.

Boy-crazy

For most of my childhood I was a tomboy. I wanted to *be* a boy. But around age eleven (near when I started to menstruate) something changed. From then on, I was boy-crazy.

Yes, there was a string of boyfriends, all but one boys from church. The odd boyfriend was Jewish. He told me he was a mystic, and I was hooked on him for most of high school.

Finally I let go of him and married a nice Episcopal boy from Sheboygan, who wanted to be a priest. He went to seminary but quit after two years. We moved to Vermont and pretty much gave up church in favor of homesteading. My Father-God love affair went dormant until my spiritual awakening at thirty-seven.

The Affair

Thirty-seven, the age when they say a woman's sexual energy is at its peak. At thirty-seven I ran into a man who knocked my socks off. He was fifty-six, Oxford educated, tall, slim and beautiful. It was the perfect setup: I'd grown up belonging to the *Church of England*, we were *living in England* at the time, and he was Scottish (close enough). I was coming home. Actually, I was unimpressed by him at the seminar where we met, until we danced together. Dancing, I looked into his eyes and a voice said 'THIS IS THE ONE.' The final chapter of the Father God Affair had begun.

The previous night in a dream I watched a young male co-worker drink all the poison in a small black medicine bottle. It was bee sting venom. He drank it and we all knew he would act crazy for some time afterwards, endangering the young 'retarded' people in our care. Other co-workers and I tried to lock him inside 'headquarters', a small multi-sided glass house. My (then) husband and I ran around trying to gather up all the keys to make sure the young co-worker would not get out. Just as we thought we had them all, an old man and a young man drove up to the glass house headquarters in a convertible sports car, bringing handfuls of keys. I knew then that my task was hopeless. Keys were everywhere.

We only had one night together, about a month after the seminar. We rode through the dark on his motorcycle, out into the English countryside where he lived alone in a stone cottage. Later that night making love, the boundaries of my personal identity were forever destroyed, not by abuse and violation, but by ecstasy.

That night I merged in ecstasy with the Father God. For the first time there were no boundaries, no rules, no expectations. For the first time in my life I experienced the flow of the cosmos *in my body*. Like water flowing in a river, so simple, so beautiful, so *un-planned*. It was a revelation to me to realize I did not have to think of doing something before actually doing it, that action, *right* action, could flow from moment to moment naturally. I remember wondering what it would be like if all of my life were to flow as easily as our lovemaking. Unbeknownst to me at the time, that query became my quest and practice for the remainder of my life, to be in touch with and to flow with the natural movement of life.

That night marked a radical departure from life as I had known it. For one thing, it was the first time I had been unfaithful to my husband of sixteen years. Second, although I had always been orgasmic I had previously thought sex was mainly about having orgasms, often working hard to have two when my husband and I made love. That night to my surprise orgasm happened all over my body, wherever we would touch. The energy between us was so strong both sexually and spiritually that wherever consciousness was focused by touch, a whirling happened. Toward morning we looked through each other's eyes in naked awe. "I am you. You am me."

Being Nobody

> *"I'm Nobody; who are you?"*
>
> *- Emily Dickinson*

The intensity of my experience with the Father God Lover resulted in my becoming totally identified with him. I let drop my old stodgy personality, the one with so many rules and prohibitions, in favor of the image of myself as his cosmic lover. I could literally (sometimes joyfully) feel chunks of my personality falling away like boulders from a rumbling mountainside as my old misconceptions of what it meant to be alive fell at the feet of the New God – Ecstasy – and his human representative, Alick.

Unfortunately for me, my projections onto this multi-orgasmic Father God figure were my private property. I *think* he tried to let me down gently. I remember it took awhile for me to get the message. Finally it got through to me that HE DIDN'T WANT ME. I was stunned. I was, at this point, not the woman I had been before, the dutiful good girl, daughter, wife and mother. And suddenly I no longer had 'Him' to mirror the newly emerging possibilities.

I was no longer His Lover. I was nobody.

I was nobody because my entire previous identity had been based upon conforming to others' expectations of who I should be, how I should behave. I had been very good at it.

It was as though in that one night I allowed a crack in my bucket of false self. *The crack in the bucket of false self.* I saw it. It was false and I would never be able to use it again.

Synopsis:

very young virgin

(age 37, married, two kids)

seeking God, beds him.

Gets ecstasy unparalleled.

Dies.

Seed planted by God sprouts.

Who is this chick, anyway?

I remember lying curled in fetal position, catatonic, on the floor of the bedroom of our lovely rented flat, a sky-dome atop a 300-year-old English country estate outside Bath. I lay there for several days, unable to motivate myself to talk or eat or change rumpled clothing. My husband talked of mental hospitals. I was afraid. Mostly I was afraid I would go insane. I was caught in my fear until the moment I realized I had a choice: I could go insane and let others take over my life for me, or I could stick with myself, my tiny embryonic totally unknown brand new shred of self, and let it take me into the uncharted territory that was sure to lie ahead. Once I saw clearly that the second choice would be more difficult, I took it without hesitation.

VOMITTING WOMAN

I feel as though I am fighting my way out from under a blanket of lies, an old crusty many-layered stinking blanket that I have been taught to believe is *protecting* me – from what? From naked truths, from feeling the cold, from breathing fresh air freely, from smelling the flowers, from touching the Earth with my bare feet.

> <u>Dream</u>: *I am a Native American woman moving around a campfire on the Plains. I am dressed in buckskin, my dark hair in two braids. I am alone. I begin vomiting and vomiting, vomiting up poison fed to me as lies against myself. I gather up the body of lies, chop it into small pieces, pound the pieces into chips. I dry the chips in the purifying sun and grind them into meal, transforming them into nourishing food and seed for my people. I offer cornmeal to the four directions.*

I will transform those lies so my daughter will not have to believe in them.

Lie #1: Girls are not as good as boys because God is male.

Lie #2: Sex is bad for you, dangerous.

Lie #3: It is ugly to be old.

Lie #4: No man will want me if I do not appear young and beautiful.

Lie #5: My most important attribute is to be attractive to men.

Lie #6: It is dangerous to show my true self.

Thoughts while cleaning house:

I keep thinking we must, as a world culture, clean up our act. We are all survivors, children of dysfunctional families and dysfunctional societies. It is no coincidence that so many of us are discovering our personal past and healing the wounds received in childhood from misguided and fragmented parents, who did the best they could. We are all survivors of 3,000 to 4,000 years of Patriarchy. We are all survivors, perpetrators and victims simultaneously of governments and businesses that lie to us for their personal, financial and political gain.

The work of therapy is to understand our personal wounding so that we may heal from the inside out. We must return the stones to their proper places in our house-of-self to make the foundations strong again. In the painful and personal process of therapy we remove the blinders so we can have a chance at becoming fulfilled human beings with wisdom and vision, living to our fullest unique creative potential.

Our society-wide work is to re-examine our cultural histories, to discover our mistaken assumptions, and to admit our mistakes. It is very important that the collective entities responsible for the damage take steps to un-tell the lies, atone for past sins and begin to re-chart the course of our group drama in light of past errors. The Christian concepts of confession, repentance (meaning to re-think), atonement and forgiveness are all brought to mind.

The personal and societal healing processes are similar in that they both involve re-examining the past for clues to what went wrong and why things went wrong. To fail to go through the healing process is to be committed to blundering on blindly and dangerously. It is to be committed to remaining a child.

Re-examining the *why*, feeling the pain of past policies and owning up to the suffering caused is essential because without unearthing the root, the weed will re-sprout, perhaps in a new location or with new clothes, but it will re-sprout and grow. The root, the deep reasons behind our policies must be understood. The foundation must be shaken.

Why we are destroying our Ecosystems

> *"Indigenous Peoples recognize their interdependence with all of creation, and they honor it...They value nature as they value their own souls. They value the earth as they value their mother."*
>
> ~Kenny Ausubel, founder, Seeds of Change

Why are we destroying our ecosystem?

Because we hate ourselves.

Why do we hate ourselves?

Because our God hates humans: they are inferior, they sin, they are stupid, they have bodies.

Because it is not safe in this world to love ourselves. Because no one ever taught us to love ourselves.

Because we come from woman.

Being a fetus in the womb.

Swimming in the warm amniotic sea

Lulled by rhythmic heartbeats and soft gurglings.

Mmmmmmmmmmmmm.

Our first pleasure-bond is with Mother. For our first nine months we are loved and protected by our mother's soft and nurturing body. Presumably it feels good in there and we only come out when we grow too big to fit comfortably. After our physical emerging, comfort, nourishment and pleasure are provided by our mother's body as she holds us, sings to us, feeds us sweet milk from the generosity of her breasts. The total body pleasure of an infant at the breast is unmistakable. Our first profound experience of pleasure is in our bodies and in relation to our mother's body. Yet as we grow we receive messages from our culture about the inferiority of the feminine and of women in general. Deep-seated confusion results from the conflict between early love and pleasure experiences and later feelings of denial and shame associated with pleasure, sex and Body.

If our society and especially our religions teach us to hate and fear the feminine principle we begin to hate and fear the part of ourselves that is bonded with women, with pleasure, with earth, with home, the part that is bonded with and connected to physical life. The mother provides the vehicle for the soul to incarnate. The mother is therefore associated with incarnation and with connection to the planet. If we are busy denying our connectedness to the feminine principle then we naturally feel disconnected from the Earth, disembodied. No feeling bond with the Divine Mother equals no feeling bond with Earth.

How can we possibly feel whole with such profound misgivings about the source of our physical being?

> Heaps of lies
>
> Heaps of lies
>
> Like autumn leaves piled sodden
>
> their numbers beyond counting.
>
> And i am an earthworm
>
> trying to eat my way through to the sun.
>
> God help me.

Friday, January 13, 1995

I must tell you that Goddess is very real for me.
Very, very real.
It was She who was there for me
when the bottom fell out,
when there was no HE to be found.
You see, I had been following 'He' around like a lovesick puppy
for most of my 37 years
in one way or another.
Always I looked up for Him or him (same thing)
always seeking the upward path toward Spirit, the Light.
I was, after all, 'on the spiritual path.' ↑ ONE WAY.
Then the bottom fell out
and He was nowhere to be found.
Apparently
He does not inhabit the bottomland.
I fell and fell through the thin air
and then into the salt sea and through the sea
to the dark NOWHERE place.
And She was there.
I met Her, and she cared for me, in her lap, the tiny me
That nobody had ever seen before.
And She allowed me to grow
at my own pace
into MY OWN WOMANNESS.

She is black
She is naked
and She has huge glist'ning thighs.
She is silent.
She loves me because I,
in my essence,
am just like her.
I love her with my life.

goddess statuette by Phillipa Bowers

Chapter Eight

Goddess

Goddess is a Verb

The Goddess is the personification of the divine feminine. She lives in every one of us, men, women and children, plants, animals, rocks, water, everything. She is the flow; whatever that means to you, she is the flow.

Once again the feminine plays opposite the masculine, for while it is held that there is only one God, there are multitudinous expressions of Goddess. As far as I can tell, there are always multiple manifestations of the She.

My friend Willow LaMonte says Goddess is a verb.

"I Goddess

you Goddess

we Goddess" and so on.

To Goddess is to recognize feminine divinity in your personal self.

Goddessing is fun. You don't have to pass any tests or memorize anything. You just have to recognize your own sacred beingness. Every woman inhabits the body of the Goddess as She moves from maiden to mother to crone. *Her* body blossoms: our body blossoms. *Her* body gives birth: our body gives birth. *Her* body ages: our body ages. It's really rather awesome. Way cool, as Willow would say.

FAX to Bethlehem *(Christmas postage stamp, 1994)*

[Postage stamp: CHRISTMAS 29 USA — Elisabetta Sirani, 1663, National Museum of Women in the Arts]

Mary, Mary, what happened to you?

I'm so sorry.

Was it a boy you were in love with?

Did you get raped?

Or was it (God, I can't even say it)
> was it your FATHER?

Oh, Mary
> you must be so ashamed.

And they made you ride on a donkey!

Nine months pregnant riding on a donkey – is this a bad joke?

And they separated you from everything familiar

made you leave home and comfort so Joseph could *pay taxes*?

No sisters, no mother, no aunties to soothe your pains and bring you tea,

to wash the child, to tell you everything would be *all right*.

You must have been so scared.

Mary, how could they *do* that to you?

I get it. That was the beginning.

After they did it to YOU, the mother of God, made *you* the lowest of the low, isolated and penniless, that made it okay to do it to the rest of us.

Mary, I'm so sorry. I'm sorry I've never loved you before. I didn't love you because it was obvious God didn't love you.

(He loved your baby but not you.)

I was so blind.

Mary, I will never again leave you.

Love, Caitlin

"Oh, Mary don't ya weep, don't ya mourn..."

"But Mary kept all these things, pondering them in her heart."
  - Luke 1:19

I grew up Episcopalian, and like most Protestants, didn't think much about Mary. I always looked down on the Catholic veneration of Mary as distasteful or crude. Doing Goddess work I gradually opened to Mary, but it wasn't until I wrote the above poem in 1995 that I connected with her personally. I realize now there is a whole lot more to Mary than the way she is represented in the poem. An English friend had this to say of her experience of Mary:

131

"My feelings went back to a little Breton church and the feast of St. Anne (Mary's mother – same difference) and there were all these women jam packed into the church, praying and chanting, and it was all to the Goddess, of course. And that is part of the story – that they can relate to this perfectly ordinary woman who took the form of a peasant girl, and the donkey ride and all the difficulties and the birth (I'll bet she wasn't all alone and without help from women really) and the alienation, etc. Not to mention the pain of a dead son, AND she suffered in poverty and was married to a boring old man and then – WOW – she gets to be Queen of Heaven crowned with stars – so she is not only Earth Goddess but Sky Goddess, too – – that is one powerful Momma."
                          A letter from Anna Gahlin 1/22/95

This is the text and poster from a lecture I gave in Brattleboro, Vermont, in 1996 in conjunction with an exhibit called "Sacred and Profane" at the Windham Gallery.

Lecture:

How the *Most Sacred* Was Turned into the Most Profane

or

"The Blackening of the Great Goddess in Europe"

Before the Christian era in Europe, the Celts and other indigenous European peoples worshipped a number of gods and goddesses. Their names varied with locale and custom, but it is safe to say that everywhere the major supporting deity was female. In Malta great stone tomb/temples were built in the shape of her bounteous body, the entry and exit between her legs. Scotland and Scandinavia were named after Skadi, a formidable dark Earth-mother type goddess related to the Indian goddess Kali.

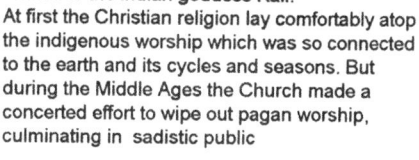

At first the Christian religion lay comfortably atop the indigenous worship which was so connected to the earth and its cycles and seasons. But during the Middle Ages the Church made a concerted effort to wipe out pagan worship, culminating in sadistic public

... culminating in sadistic public torture and murder of hundreds of thousands who clung to the old ways. Symbols and ideas that had been the most sacred to the old religion became the most profane to the new. Women's status is perhaps the most obvious reversal, along with the concept of sex as sacred. But old ways die hard, therefore they can often be rooted out by

133

imaginative research. Remnants always seem to survive in the form of superstition, folklore and folk customs. Prohibitions and reversals are a good place to start looking.

For example, Friday was named for Freya, the Norse Goddess of dance and song. Her day along with her special number thirteen (the number of moon cycles in one year) went from being the luckiest day to the unluckiest. In 1980 a fiercely proud Vermonter, a former school teacher living in the farmhouse where she was born around 1900, told me in no uncertain terms that she never started anything new on a Friday, Fridays being the 'bad' day of the week.

My beloved grandmother, born in 1900 to a proper English mother, was not allowed to whistle as a child because "girls weren't supposed to whistle." Was it because Bridget, triple Goddess of the Northern Isles, taught a mysterious whistling language to her priestesses, who used it to communicate across those green hills and vales? There was probably a time in the British Isles when it was downright dangerous for a girl to whistle.

It surely was dangerous to be a midwife, healer or herbalist for many centuries. My friend Elise wonders if her mother's near hysterical insistence upon removing 'weeds' from around the house might be a remnant from a time long ago when it was not safe to have dandelion and other medicinal herbs growing near the family dwelling place.

I am grateful to have the freedom to whistle, to grow and use healing herbs and to enjoy Fridays. I am grateful that Goddess is once again spiraling out of the closet as circles of women laugh and chant and dance together, rebirthing the Sacred Feminine.

Chapter Nine

Emotions

<u>The Scene of the Holy Play</u>   January 3, 1991

The sacred body, the seat of the soul, the scene of the HOLY PLAY is YOU and ME. I know now that the concept of Sacred Earth will not take hold unless and until the beholder can experience his/her *body as sacred*.

We have been cut off from earth, from roots, from body. We strive for spiritual enlightenment because we have no security, no place to stand, no base. We are orphans; we cannot be wholly spiritual because we have these messy dirty bodies, so we hate our bodies and try to deny their existence. This particular denial cuts us off from our spiritual mother and from the earthy, pleasurable reality of eating and defecating and making love. We are caught agonizing in the middle, like Jesus on the cross.

Rembrandt, 1563

Every act, every creation is the sacred enactment of a god, acting through us. This is god as archetype, not 'good' or 'bad' gods, but gods as different aspects of energies present in us all. It's like a deck of cards or a painter's palette, it is 'what we are made of', our recipe for Earth's creatures, just as the table of elements includes all the physical building blocks of the known universe.

I am after the emotional building blocks of the known universe.

The Dance of Life is expressed by molecules, colors, the stream, the tree, the sky, the temper-tantrum, the television, the life cycles of us all, the seasonal cycles. All are the Dance, and all are by definition SACRED.

When I feel this, I feel small and awed, but a comfortable small, a fitting-in small, a miraculous dancing small perfect/imperfect one-in-a-trillion tiny/huge perfect imperfections,

ALL DANCING.

Emotions and the Body

"We are the Universe experiencing its own magnificence."
- Val Silidker, Awaken to Wholeness Summit

My body
    I can't tell you
        how important
            she is
                to
                    me.

She is the seat

of my soul.

My emotions

emit

from my pores.

Cellular, glandular, hormonal secretions make physical

that which is ephemeral.

A thought, a feeling translates into action, into tears manufactured by cells who deal in such delicate matters,

cells who KNOW that when it is time to cry they must crank up the pistons, start the engine and secrete the 'secret' secretions.

The emotions – where are they?

The imagination –

    Where hides the myth in the body?

> *"A disembodied emotion is a sheer nonentity."*
>   ~William James
>
> *"It is impossible to separate body and emotions."*
>   ~Clyde Ford

    The lens through which we view the world is focused by the senses and interpreted by the mind, but the body of the telescope is made of emotions. People may think differently according to their culture and personal histories, but all people have emotions in common.

RAGE   FEAR

Grief   JOY   *I feel them in my body,*
I feel them in my body.

Our emotions inform our truth. Emotions come first, before belief, before thought. They are the basis upon which our beliefs are built, our myths being the stories we tell ourselves in order to make sense of the world around us.

Recent research in the field of psychoneuroimmunology confirms William James' century-old theory that bodily changes arising in response to a particular situation *give rise to* emotions. This is to say that the 'bodily events' come first, followed by the awareness of the bodily events, and then the emotion is registered in the brain *as a result of awareness of the body's responses.*

Dr. Clyde Ford, chiropractor, psychotherapist and author of several books on the role of human touch in healing and recovery, agrees with James that 'bodily changes do precede emotional experience." Ford goes on to say that memory of emotional trauma is stored in the body and can be retrieved and healed through compassionate touch. It is a relief to know that we are open systems and can heal our emotional as well as our physical wounds if we apply our own loving awareness.

The War Between Mind and Body

If the head is analogous to waking consciousness, then the rest of the body is analogous to the unconscious. I don't claim to understand exactly how it works, but in some way the body acts as a representative of the unconscious mind. Arnold Mindell's wonderful work with the 'dream body' is based upon a similar understanding of the mind/body, conscious/unconscious correlation.

We are familiar with the conscious mind as decision-maker, planner and thinker, the one who has ideas that the body is then supposed to carry out. The *un*conscious mind seems full of fears and contradictions, sometimes acting as spoiler of our best-laid plans by surprising us with hidden resistance. Often the mind and body seem to have different agendas. When my lower back went out *before* I started packing for an important move, I knew I needed to stop and deal with my emotional reactions to the move before my body would let me get on with it. Chronically overweight dieters and unhappy smokers attest to the fact that unconscious desires frequently overrule conscious intentions.

Our intentions may be above board and honorable, but often our motives lie hidden in unconscious territory.

I had a serious conflict with a woman whose actions precipitated in me a great deal of personal pain and even humiliation. "It couldn't be my fault that you are feeling hurt, because I didn't intend to hurt you," she insisted. While her (conscious) intentions may have been good, I believe that her (unconscious) motives ruled her actions. She said her 'spirit guides' were telling her what to do. What were her motives? I can only guess.

Motive = motion. E-motion. What motivates us is what actually *moves* our physical body, causing us to act in the world. As we bridge the gap between conscious and unconscious we gradually come to befriend our unconscious aspects, allowing our actions and emotions to come more closely into alignment with our intentions. This process is called integration.

Caitlin's most valuable advice:

Stop & feel it.

Whatever it is, when you become aware of a feeling inside, you must STOP.

Ask yourself "What am I feeling?" Then simply allow yourself to

FEEL.

The feeling will instruct you.

It is a gift from your innermost self. If you want to be a whole person, it is imperative to honor those most intimate gifts. FEEL.

FEEL, FEEL, FEEL. Then breathe, and continue with your day, enriched for having touched in with your own truth.

Feeling is an excellent use of your time on the meditation cushion. Sit. Close your eyes. What is here to feel? Feel it. Let the body process the feelings (it can take several minutes, maybe longer). Come to peace naturally, after the wave has passed. You say you want emotional health? This practice is a requirement. Scared at the thought of doing it? Heed my first therapists's wise words: "A feeling never killed anyone." Feel.

Authentic Movement

The practice of Authentic Movement has contributed immeasurably to my understanding of my body's (unconscious) mind.

Authentic Movement involves a 'witness' and a 'mover.' The mover closes her eyes and moves *in any way she pleases,* while the witness watches quietly with full, nonjudgmental attention. That's all. When the mover finishes the two may talk about their experience or they may not. Authentic Movement is not about talking, it's about moving from the source. It's about re-moving the head, so to speak, demoting the judge who lives in our head, and letting the body speak unfettered. The body has stories of its own to tell. Authentic Movement is a very simple and profound healing technique for body and soul because it gives the unconscious material a way to surface and be witnessed by the conscious mind *in a nonjudgmental context.* Gradually the mover develops an inner witness for herself, modeled on the outer witness.

Authentic Movement sets up a dialogue between conscious and unconscious, mind and body, intention and motive, a dialogue that short-circuits our ingrained cultural habit of censure. If as children we were disapproved of for being emotional or spontaneous or for acting in certain ways, we internalize disapproval and perpetuate the top-down chain of command. The head says to the body as the adult said to the child "You will behave," "You will not cry when you are hurt or sad," (especially if you are a boy), or "You will not show your anger" (especially if you are a girl).

The top-down chain of command serves to keep the body-knowing in an inferior position, like a child who is sometimes naughty, or a slave who must obey orders. A top-down chain of command forces the body-knowing into hiding so it has to sneak around to get its needs met unbeknownst to the disapproving judge/parent who lives on top of the neck.

Authentic Movement, by allowing the unconscious to speak through the body, encourages the creative soul to come out of hiding and share both its pain and its marvelous joy. The natural dialogue, the flow between body-knowing and mind-knowing that was natural to us as children and is the hallmark of integrated creative adults, is reestablished. The mover begins to trust her body-knowing to lead her in the right direction in life. The 'judge' begins to let go its iron grip. Joy becomes a more frequent visitor as the natural free flowing of life is resumed.

<u>Body Logic</u>

"Paying close attention" is an opening of the mind to present experience – the female complement of the male 'need to know'. By fostering an alert sensitivity to all the changes and exchanges precipitated by your breathing, and to the orchestration of energy as it waxes and wanes through the scalp and jaw and throat and shoulders and pelvis and legs and ankles – by simply receiving all of those sensations of the flesh and paying close attention to them, you will release

endarkening tensions, open the body's mindfulness, and eventually settle into a sense of being sensationally present. You may even feel your consciousness sift down to the core of your being and come to rest in the pelvic bowl – inspiring the simple, joyous recognition, "here I am." At that point what you are feeling is not just the body, but the self; you are feeling the coursing resolution of who you are, clear and grounded and at ease in the transforming present; you are "feeling the thing as a whole."

~ *Phillip Shepherd,* <u>New Self, New World</u>

Some characterize emotional response as irrational, but I find the body to have perfect logic, always based on its direct personal experience. It is not the body/mind but the conscious mind that is able to make dramatic illogical leaps. The body is always grounded in direct experience.

The body has a logic of its own.
The body doesn't think, it feels.
And like an elephant, it never forgets.

Harville Hendrix says the emotional body "has no sense of linear time. Understanding this basic fact about the nature of your unconscious may explain why you sometimes have feelings that seem alarmingly out of proportion to the events that triggered them." Memories of trauma are stored in the body and when a situation arises that mimics the original trauma in some key way, the body catapults the person into the stew of images and feelings present at the original trauma. Usually people are not consciously aware of the link with the original trauma, either because it occurred in early childhood before cognitive memory and language skills were learned, or because the brain often blocks memories of traumatic events. This explains why Susan always feels like crying when anyone criticizes her – she was reacting as she did as a child when her parents and teachers criticized her. She felt helpless and worthless. The 'emotional body' remembered and overruled her conscious adult desire to control her emotional responses.

Robert wanted to be physically intimate with women, but felt overcome with irrational fear at being in bed with a woman. With the help of a therapist, he was able to remember sexual abuse suffered in infancy in the bed of his adoptive mother. The body remembers. The body is perfectly logical and often will not allow normal functioning until the emotional wound is uncovered and healed.

A child-molester promises never to do it again. He sincerely wants (consciously) to never harm another child. But when he gets near children of a certain age, his body remembers how his own innocence was stolen by an uncle. His body wants so badly to re-experience its own innocence that he steals the innocence of a child in an attempt to reclaim his own.

The body remembers.
The body is perfectly logical in its own way.

Very often the body can give us valuable insights that are unavailable to the conscious mind. Self-compassion is awakened and strengthened by this work.

Mind Games

Cyberspace – unlimited possibilities – the quintessential mind-game of our age. Contrast cyberspace and its 'unlimited possibilities' with our finite bodies. We each have only one and it's made to last one human lifetime. It is very small at first, takes fourteen to twenty-five years to reach full size and function. After forty years or so it begins to show signs of wear. By sixty it is noticeably slowing down, and by eighty the mind may still be sharp if you're lucky, but the body is definitely on its way out.

Unlimited? I think not. At times it seems like there's a war going on between the mind with its need to dream and the body with its need to be healthy. Integration of mind and body leads to wholeness.

As a culture we have been in love with the soaring limitless expansiveness of the Mind Game since the days of Classical Greece. For this game the mind is on the *top*, in the *superior* position. Concepts associated with mind are:

head

up

limitless

forever

logical thinking

conscious

brain

clarity

smart

At odds with the Mind Game is the Body Game. The Body Game is *below*, in the *inferior* position. Concepts associated with body are:

body (below the head)

down

limited

finite

unconscious

emotional

irrational

hidden

dumb

Speaking somewhat simplistically, the mind doesn't like the body because it cramps its style. The body imposes LIMITS to what the mind can do. The nature of the mind is limit*less*. The nature of the body is limit*ed*. In a culture where mind is Boss, body becomes the flunky, reminding us of our limitations. Limitation feels like a bad thing. Denial becomes the order of the day.

Denial Games

"Men in Suits"

My view is right.

Despite evidence to the contrary…..

I insist

we create our own reality, don't we?

I wish it, therefore

The emperor is wearing a suit of the finest rarest gold thread.

I say so, therefore…

He……experts attest…..

The electorate says….the newspapers…

……advertisers acclaim…..

the suit is extraordinary…..

….gold and

I say! – therefore

I think I am.

So it becomes, once you can see it, a tyranny presided over by the mind-gamers, in love with linear top-down thinking. But once we begin to take off our blinders and see that the emperor is not wearing any clothes at all, we begin to question the whole top-down perspective. If the emperor isn't wearing clothes, then maybe there are other policies we might wish to reconsider.

Maybe if the body has its own logic based upon its own experiential history, and if the body is the only vehicle that can carry out the schemes of the mind, maybe it would be to the advantage of the mind in the long run to listen to the body, to its piece of the truth, before proceeding with plans.

Simple.

If the body holds its own logical well-founded truth, and if the mind needs the body in order to act in the world, wouldn't it make sense to take on the body AS PARTNER rather than slave?

When the body holds the key to the limits to growth, wouldn't it make sense to ask it to communicate its truth so the captain (the conscious mind) can know in which direction to set sail? Wouldn't we be more likely to reach our destination if we have all hands on deck?

With the evolutionary stage of human consciousness called Patriarchy came a set of values that informed the choices we made as a culture. These values came from the mind and are based on hierarchy: a linear, top-down organizational hierarchy, a linear way of thinking that gradually won over the cyclical, circular way of *being* personified in earlier developmental stages of human consciousness.

Progression:

Dream of Animals: consciousness undifferentiated from Nature

Birth of Humans: (Paleolithic) Human species differentiates itself through naming and separating from nature. Gods are created to express awe and bliss, the two basic emotional polarities.

Childhood: (Neolithic) Development of circular/cyclical consciousness. Seasons, agriculture. With the Mother. Tribal awareness. Creating culture and agriculture further separates humans from Nature.

Adolescence: (Patriarchal) Development of linear consciousness. With the Father. Emergence of the individual. Hierarchical, linear thinking.

The end of adolescence is where we find ourselves now, moving through a treacherous passage into adulthood.

One of the problems with linear consciousness is that someone has to be on the top and someone else has to be on the bottom. Peter and I had a party one summer to inaugurate our council drum. It was held in the forest, with drumming and dancing in a circle. Our neighbor brought her guest, a recent immigrant from Europe who was a Christian fundamentalist. We asked him to join us, but he declined, saying *it was against his religion to gather in circles*. This seems a particularly clear illustration of concretization of values into rules of conduct. His religion rejects gathering in circles because circles illustrate equality. In a circle no one is obviously more or less important than anyone else. The circle negates linear consciousness.

We have been living with a system of linear consciousness that values

> brain over body
>
> heaven over earth
>
> boss over workers
>
> thinking over feeling
>
> men over women
>
> humans over plants and animals
>
> product over process
>
> etc. etc. etc.

Linear consciousness is an understandable and forgivable misconception, given our species' infatuation with mind games, but at this moment in history it is no longer viable. Indeed, reliance upon linear consciousness threatens our very existence.

Our collective *body* is telling us it is time for a shift. Our collective *body* (physical fact) is telling us the Earth is a finite sphere with finite resources. We ignore this intelligence at our peril.

Our collective body is telling us it has its own piece of the truth and if we continue to ignore its message it will simply stop cooperating. It will make us sick. By making us sick it will bring us the gift of awareness of our limits, the physical limitations imposed by the fact that our consciousness is blessed and cursed with being housed in a vulnerable imperfect physical body on a Living Earth, our larger body, that has finite shape, form, function and resources.

"I think, therefore I am," said Rene Descartes. "Well, not quite," I like to say. But that statement tells us a lot about the state of mind of the thinker. The heady power of creating from the mind (imagination) has informed the linear consciousness that characterizes our age, to the point where

Descartes believed his very existence depended upon thinking.

My body would laugh at the absurdity, at the sheer irrational arrogance of this 'thought.' It would, that is, if it were not suffering from the polluting effects of the mind's intoxication.

Obviously the thinker believes his statement to be true. He has, in fact, a whole belief system that supports his conclusion. But the *experience,* the physical experience of his body belies it. Alas, the emperor is wearing no clothes at all.

Bliss and Awe

> *"Wonder is my watchword," says Peter.*
> *"Bliss is our natural state," says Caitlin.*
> *"Life is movement," says Gabrielle Roth.*

Bliss and awe (or wonder) are the two fundamental emotional states associated with spiritual experience.

> bliss and awe
> attraction and retreat
> celebration and wonder
> participation and observation

Bliss describes the emotional aspect of perfect union with the beloved. It is illustrated and characterized by a baby at the breast, and by rare moments during lovemaking. Bliss is the sensation of being totally at rest in perfect union with the beloved, a sense of being *at one*. Joseph Campbell says "when one can feel oneself in relation to the universe in the same complete and natural way as that of the child with the mother, one is in complete harmony and tune with the universe." Bliss is our natural state.

Awe requires being separate from the beloved. Awe can be illustrated and characterized by a person looking up at the star-filled night sky. Awe is the act of being a loving observer of the immensity of that which is outside one's self. One cannot feel awe or wonder unless one feels separate from and less than. Simply put: awe requires being away from; bliss requires being united. Both involve love. Awe contains an element of fear, but an exciting and challenging kind of fear, like that of a mountain climber looking at a mountain peak he is about to attempt to scale.

Desire is what causes movement either toward or away from the states of bliss and awe. All life reflects and enacts the play of opposites in every dimension. Desire for union (bliss) inspires movement toward. Desire for observation, contemplation and individuation (awe) inspires movement away from.

Dual desires are expressed in an 18-month-old child, toddling alternately toward and away from its mother. Both desires are strong in children of this age as they experiment with letting go of Mom's apron strings for just a few moments, a coy game of visual hide and seek. It is inevitably an 18-month-old, two-foot-tall stranger whom you will discover hugging your leg in a crowd, until she looks up and sees the wrong face at the top of the leg. Uh, oh!

As an adult I have felt the warring of dual desires when I travel to exotic places: a desire to be totally *in* the experience, and a simultaneous desire to observe and record it with my camera. A desire to be at one with, and a desire to step out of (to be 'two' with) the experience, to contemplate its significance. Jungian wise-woman Edith Sullwold told me 'two' represents coming to consciousness, because 'one' cannot know itself. Only by breaking from oneness and becoming two is consciousness born because then one has something with which to compare itself. The 18-month-old is discovering her ability to be a discreet individual, to be not-merged with Mama. The blissful mother-infant pair is splitting so that the consciousness of the child can be born.

Ecstasy and Religion

Ex stasis: out of the normal state
Religio: to tie back

Ecstasy is an intense emotional state that includes aspects of both bliss and awe. The impulse for religion, all religion, comes from the need to safely experience ecstasy. Shamans, priests and priestesses are specialists in ecstasy, guides whose job is to provide a shepherded safe ecstatic experience for their group. Religion is a way to tie everyone in the group together by sharing an intense primal ecstatic experience. Locations for ritual are chosen or specially built for their ability to heighten the desired effect. From Paleolithic caves in Spain and France to Chartres Cathedral is really a very short hop. Traditional tools used by 'ritual guides' around the world are music, drumming, dance, fasting, image and symbol, fire and light, and consecrated food.

Tribal cultures celebrated the adolescent's entry into adulthood by initiating young men and women into tribally-sanctioned ecstatic experience such as first intercourse, hallucinogenic substances administered by elders, and participation in trance dance. The plus side of taking on adult responsibility in the tribe is to be allowed to participate in ecstatic ritual. How your tribe got ecstasy defined your tribe's religious experience.

The Shakers, an industrious agrarian religious sect popular in 19th century America, disallowed virtually all private contact between men and women, including sexual relations between married couples. They provided plenty of ecstasy, however, during evening prayer meetings when members would dance and sing and shake ecstatically with the spirit, men on one side of the room and women on the other side.

Certain Christian denominations provide only awe, promising followers bliss after death if they will forgo experiencing ecstasy in life: no drugs or alcohol, very restricted sex, no card-playing, no dancing and so on. Delay of permission for ecstasy can be interpreted as delay of permission to enter adulthood, in effect a delay of initiation into the tribe until after death. Christian iconography, particularly scenes of Jesus on the cross, often portray death as the ultimate ecstatic experience, the long-awaited moment of initiation when one is finally judged worthy to join with one's god in the after-life.

In Goddess religions, the emphasis is on bliss. The Goddess is *in* all creation. Everything and everyone is of and from the body of the Great Mother. Women personify the Goddess. Men are her sons and lovers, totally connected and surrounded by her, but *lesser than,* as a child in the womb is lesser than the mother who surrounds and creates it. Important in goddess religions are *circles,* equality, joy, acceptance, inclusion. *Here* and *now* are emphasized.

In the bachelor-God religions, the emphasis is on awe. God is *separate* from his creation. God is *above;* everything else is *below.* According to what I learned in Sunday School, humans are born in sin and live always in sin, a state of separation from God. Past (what is written in the Bible) and future (life after death) are more important than this life. In the traditional order, women are lesser than men who are lesser than God. Science was the child of this kind of linear thinking, sprung out of the head of the bachelor God. Without linear separationist thinking, science and the exploration of our world in an objective way would be unthinkable. Thus male-centric religions allowed human beings to further individuate and differentiate ourselves from our surroundings. We are able to see and experience, manipulate and exploit the world as we do only because we are able to distinguish ourselves as separate from it through the example of a god who is separate from his creation.

Both female-centric and male-centric religions have crystallized a piece of the truth, but both gaze mainly at one of the poles of experience, ignoring the other. The truth includes both poles and is the movement (the PLAY) between them. The *life* is in the alternation between polarities.

ALIVE: The Dance of Wave and Particle

Light waves: disappearing reappearing disappearing reappearing
Molecules: unforming reforming unforming reforming
moment by moment
breathing in, breathing out
form and formlessness forming formless you and me.
Form at heart IS formless.
How to express it except to say that the one IS
(contains the entirety of) the other?
Alternating current AC:
the power is in the alternation, the pull between polarities,
the constant inconstancy.

To fail to see and embrace inconstancy is to be frozen by fear to the illusion
of permanence.
Thus frozen we are thrust into insecurity.
We panic
at the perceived threat
of formlessness.
Grab it! STOP IT!
Make it STAY!
Grabbing at form, essence evaporates,
form becomes a lifeless shell.

BUT NOW

I AM ALIVE!

The only knowing is the knowing of one's own truth,

moment by moment.

One can't live truth retrospectively.

The only way out of the maze, the only way to not become frozen with terror

at the fluctuation between life and the seeming absence of life,

is to know who you truly are.

<u>*Here*</u> *is the only safe place, the only truth, the only home,*

the only mother

the only father

the only lover

I feel *awe* at the size of the challenge before humans today: to take responsibility collectively and individually for the God-like powers we now have, in order to allow Earth to rise once again to the revered position of Our Living Mother.

I feel *bliss* at the opportunity to be part of the solution, alive and awake at this incredible moment in our evolution, ready at the moment of initiation to do my part.

> "We are the dream of the Earth
> And we must awaken within that Dream
> By breaking the bonds of sleep.
> For awaken you must...
> For when the moment comes
> And the conductor nods your way
> Then you must act
> If the Dream of the Earth
> Is to be fulfilled."
>
> ~From a poem by Ross Jennings

The Big Picture

In the big picture, you know, the Patriarchy is not about men being the bad guys. The Patriarchy has been about all of us, men and women, playing the roles of having or not having power while we all agree to experiment with linear consciousness.

If there was a big book it might be titled <u>The Human Story: Experiments in Modes of Consciousness Available to Homo Sapiens</u>. The chapter we're now finishing would be "Linear Consciousness: the Hierarchy of the Thinking Brain." The next chapter would be "Integration of Linear and Cyclical Consciousness," we hope.

The fact that men have had dominance over women for two or three thousand years is logical given our history and gender imagery, but it is neither fundamental nor final. Men are not responsible for the evolution of the era named after God the Father any more than women are responsible for our time under the wing of the Great Mother. If you believe in reincarnation or in the existence of a collective unconscious, you can easily see that we all share in the creation of our social/emotional climate. We collaborate. Human consciousness is evolving.

The critical task before us is to stop creating animosity and polarization by blaming any one group for causing the problem. We need to see clearly what has led up to where we are now, to identify the cultural beliefs that have led us to this very sticky place. Next comes healing the past by owning up to past abuses and letting go of dysfunctional patterns and beliefs. Only with a more mature perspective can we envision and move into "the more beautiful world our hearts know is possible," as contemporary holistic philosopher Charles Eisenstein states.

> *"Thou lovest them in thy heart;*
> *born of thee, born of thee."*
> *~ hymn to a Moon Goddess, 3400 BCE*

Chapter Ten

Moving Toward Wholeness

The Stacked Deck

(note: this chapter was written in the mid-1990s. Attitudes toward women and sensitivity to gender-equality has changed for the better since that time. Let this stand as true for the time it was written, not so very long ago!)

Two common examples of the problem:

Example #1: In the autumn of 1994 the local excellent liberal arts college put on a series of presentations called "Celebrating Creativity." Out of twenty presenters, all local creative people, seventeen were male. I thought about going around town scribbling "Men's" between "Celebrating" and "Creativity" on the posters, because that's what they were doing, celebrating men's creativity. I am happy to say that in the 20+ years since then, the climate for women has improved dramatically, at least in Vermont.

Example #2: My daughter was a freshman in 1994 at another very fine liberal arts college in Vermont, formerly an all-women's college. She took a course titled "American Poetry." Seventy-five to eighty percent of the poems studied were written by men. The professor, a poet, was also a man. The course should have been called "Male Poets of America."

I don't have any objection to studying poetry by men or men's creativity, but it would be helpful to realize that the standards our culture has been using are created by and for men, so of course men measure up best. Although a smattering of exceptional women have been recognized for excelling in a man's world, one could say that in general women's special talents have been overlooked, as *men's* talents, *men's* creativity and *men's* vision have been supremely manifested during the Patriarchal era. As the quintessential manifestation of the masculine creative spirit, the Patriarchal era illustrates the pendulum swung fully opposite to the Neolithic Age of the Great Goddess, where "the full fecund energy and consciousness of universal woman is elaborated."

I doubt that the women leaders of the Neolithic realized that their culture was ignoring the masculine any more than our culture realized until recently that we have been ignoring the feminine. For the women of that distant time the feminine perspective was the only perspective of which they were aware. I don't believe they could see anything else.

The Main Problem

The number one problem is the way our culture looks at things. We have been looking at the world through men's eyes with men's values, men's perspective, with vision for men's hopes and dreams. Until recently all humanity was routinely referred to as 'mankind.'

> *"Peace on earth, Goodwill toward* **Men***"- traditional Christmas Carol*

> *"One small step for a man, a giant step for* **mankind***."*
> *– Neil Armstrong's first words as he walked on the moon, 1969*

> *The Ascent of* **Man** *– a 13-part BBC documentary from 1973, written and presented by Jacob Bronowski*

and so on.

For the four thousand years of recorded *his*-story, the overwhelming majority of our powerful people, leaders, healers, philosophers, writers, artists, musicians, explorers, athletes, have been male, so our culture has of course had a masculine perspective. The deck has been stacked. The deck is still stacked, and because it is stacked in an unbalanced way, it is about to fall over.

One important step we could take would be to recognize that there is a qualitative difference in the way women and men experience the world. Our culture has been assuming incorrectly that men's way is the *only* way, or certainly the *superior* way. If we could see that there is also women's way, if we could see that women's way is different and would lead us in a different direction, perhaps we could begin to move toward planetary healing instead of toward suicide. We are not bound to a one-sided lopsided masculinized vision of human beings' interactions with the world. We are not required to be imprisoned by the last three thousand years of the masculine experiment. We can change the course of our own cultural evolution if we can imagine the fundamental change in consciousness that is needed in order to effect the change.

How to Change

I believe the fundamental change in consciousness needed at this time is a recognition that

1. We have been seeing the world almost exclusively through masculine eyes.
2. The feminine view would give us a very different but equally valid take on the world.
3. It is absolutely essential that we explore and increasingly adopt the missing feminine perspective if we as a species expect to survive another century.

And what is the feminine perspective that we must adopt and integrate? It consists of caring, healing, wholeness. It involves taking care of those who need care, taking care of the Earth. Its qualities are listening, receiving, responding, paying attention to what is needed for health and wholeness, then giving what is needed. These are all qualities of good parenting, qualities of the heart. In effect, we must become good parents to all of Earth's children, all of them, to keep them safe and healthy and in balance with each other. Good stewardship, the bible calls it. We must let go of attachment to competition, let go of the myth of personal gain, and replace that with the truer truth that we all benefit when we are all included. This is survival, not of the lonesome individual, but of the family, of the tribe. Our tribe is the Earth.

Art Births the Artist

Creating art is a transformational act. The highest art is not about the end product, the painting or the book, the poem or musical composition, but about what happens to the artist while the work is being created. Art is the expression of the soul's imagination as it interacts with the conscious aspects of self. Art is a sacred dialogue between conscious and unconscious, embodiment and transcendence.

Art differs from craft in that art's intention is expression of the soul's journey, where craft's intention is creation of a useful or decorative object. Although objects produced by art and craft may look very similar it is the process taking place inside the mind and soul of the human that determines whether art or craft has taken place. Of course there are no firm lines of demarcation between the two.

For about three years in my early 40s I created and performed autobiographical performance art consisting of dance and spoken word. Inspiration for each piece came out of my inner well, giving body to an aspect of my personal journey through myth and allegory. Performance was a meaningful rite of passage as I shared my creative maturation process with the public, friends and family.

Creating this book has been another foray into making art that has affected me profoundly. Although much of the material for the book was gathered from journal entries written before the book was conceived, the act of preparing both old and new writings caused them to mature, taking on new layers of meaning, shape and texture. The maturing of the work caused a corresponding maturing in the writer, along with a deepening that I surely did not anticipate but for which I am deeply grateful. Writing this book gave me the opportunity to withdraw deep inside where, sheltered by my family and my beloved mentor, Edith Sullwold, I was able to create a meaningful body of work that when completed made space for movement to the next level of maturity.

I believe strongly that the emphasis of true art should not be on the product, but on the *process* of creating, which cannot help but transform the creator. In order for art to be successful on the inner planes, the artist must understand that the purpose of art is not to create objects but to communicate with inner realms in order to release and express life energy. *Objects of art are the by-products of communication with other realms.*

Art is a doorway to life's vitality. Through art one can communicate with demons that may be blocking our flow, as well as angels who can help us along and illuminate our path. Through art we make contact with ourselves so that our 'aliveness channels' become widened. The process of making art may be therapeutic, bringing painful memories up to awareness and allowing them to be seen, felt and healed. With that healing comes freedom, joy and gratitude for being alive.

Art establishes sacred communion between inner and outer. Paralleling the process of communication between individuals, self-communication leads to inner dialogue and self-understanding, making room for MORE LOVE and MORE LIFE. Boldly I say that if the artist is *not* changed in the process of making art, he/she is approaching art from the wrong direction, ending up not with art but with skill and craft.

My friend Ayla uses the phrase 'living process' to describe the daily search for a meaningful relationship to self and the world. She maintains that people can choose to be in 'living process' nearly all the time by being aware that life presents us with daily opportunities to awaken. Any place in your daily interactions where you notice discomfort is an opportunity to learn more about yourself, to practice being true and notice when you're not.

Occasionally we are led into 'deep process,' Ayla tells us, which is characterized by a very real and often difficult period of soul-searching. Art can be a doorway into deep process, if we allow it. It is perhaps easier to allow soul-dialogue through art if one has not been to art school, because of the aspect of comparison and judging that cannot be avoided in that environment.

When art is used as a medium of expression for re-experiencing the suffering of one's soul, the art becomes the embodiment of the suffering that can then be gestated, birthed and *released into the world*, making space for a whole new relationship with the world. The artist then becomes both baby (re-born into a fuller capacity for life) and mother (adult vessel) by whose physical and emotional nurturance the emergent being is allowed to come into embodiment. At this point in the process, joy is freed up to be felt and expressed.

Any art form that captures the imagination of the journeyer can be used as vehicle for the soul's journey. Art, like goddess, is a verb and must not be confused with its by-products, for no matter how lovely and captivating they may be it is the transformation of the artist that is the proper goal of true art.

Enactment as Empowerment

As a student of living culture as well as the ancient past, I have become increasingly aware of the extent to which every culture consciously or unconsciously enacts its religious beliefs. For example, our culture believes in an all-powerful male god and therefore has created CEOs and popes and presidents as its secular rulers. Another example is Bali, a jewel in the chain of islands that is Indonesia. In traditional Balinese culture, everyone got into the act. In their language, there is no word for artist because art is not separate from life. Every Balinese is an artist of one sort or another, involved in creating and enacting beauty in harmony with the spirits who inhabit their paradisiacal island. They believe in participation and harmony with Nature and each other, and that's what their culture embodies. Enactment is empowering and powerful in that it creates a visible physical reality corresponding to one's invisible beliefs.

The simplest enactment is the circle itself. A change of meeting-place format from lectern with rows of seats to a circle can cause both subtle and profound changes in the group dynamic.

It is important to take a long moment to decide what we wish to embody at this pivotal juncture in the human story. What shall we enact? May I suggest the following:

1. Stewardship of Sacred Earth.
2. Identification with all sentient beings, including Gaia.
3. Expression, recognition and embodiment of the sacred nature of our emotions, since they are rather important aspects of our divine-human nature.
4. Healthy sexuality based on love and respect for self and partner.
5. Fluid two-way relating based on expression of emotional and physical truth, emphasizing the ability to respond to changing needs as opposed to relying on quickly outmoded rigid systems of conduct.

Community enactments can be a powerful tool for cultural transformation. I do not mean putting on amusing plays, but community-performed pageants, dramas or comedies chosen for their relevance to the true-life drama we are living, the crisis of our times.

We need a beacon providing inspiration for all of us, a vision for our collective future that includes believable struggle and a believable happy ending. We need models for survival including visions of cultural wholeness as well as individual characters who model the mature integration of body and mind, masculine and feminine, etc. Starhawk's novel *The Fifth Sacred Thing* as well as the film *Avatar* are visionary works upon which group enactments might be based and like the *Mahabarata* or the Passion of Christ, could be enacted yearly in each community to fertilize and inspire the community's vision of itself moving into what is sure to be a challenging future. We need a new vision of integration and wholeness where stability and dramatic change are not opposites, but cooperating partners in a dynamic dance of wholeness and healing of the Earth.

Before we can enact a new vision of wholeness, we must make space for it in our consciousness by clearing out the old paradigms. We must bring the darkness into light by revealing and healing the ghosts of wounded children who inhabit our collective and individual psyches. We must continue as a culture the work of integration begun by Freud and Jung, because our species has evolved to the point where it needs psychological and emotional healing in order to mature and survive. After we have cleaned our psychological house, gone to the dump, had a yard-sale and a big bonfire, only then will we know what kind of unnecessary junk has been occupying significant space in our hearts and minds. Like an overloaded boat, we can't take on new cargo until the old cargo has been unloaded, item by item. Some of it we may wish to keep, but some we must surely throw away. The old myths are no longer feeding us. Quite frankly, they are sinking the ship. This is how we know it is time to take inventory.

The Bottom Line

At breakfast with Peter and my eighteen-year-old daughter, my daughter says that some of her young male friends envy women, even wishing they could *be* women.

Impassioned discussion ensued.

Agreement was reached:

Three levels of right relationship are essential* to wholeness.
1. right relation to self
2. right relation to other
3. right relation to All That Is

All three are of equal* importance.

All three must be seen as sacred* relationships.

*Definitions:

Essential *means none can be adequately achieved without the others*

Equal *means none should be seen as having priority or primacy over the others*

Sacred *means seen as emanating from the Great Mystery in which we live and breathe and have our being*

Right Relation to Self involves moving toward self-love by replacing subliminal cultural messages of self-hatred and self-ignorance with self-acceptance and self-knowing.

Its essential questions are

"Who am I?"

and parenthetically, ("Do I deserve to exist?")

Its qualities are: one, inner focus, love

Right Relation to Other (I-thou) involves relating to all others as equals who are different from you. It must be based upon respect as in "re-seeing" the value in another

165

who is unlike oneself. It includes gender relations.

Its essential questions are

> *"Who am I in relation to you?"*
> *"Who are men in relation to women?"*
> *"Who are women in relation to men?"*

Its essential qualities are: two, duality, seeing others

Right Relation to Cosmos includes our sacred relationship to Earth and the Heavens.

Its essential question is

"Who are humans in relation to everything else?"

Its essential qualities are: All, outer focus, inclusive

The Last Chapter

A Dream: I am the son in a family. The mother has long blonde hair like my sister. She sends me on an errand. I come to a tall wire enclosure on the top of a hill. There is a man inside, but he thinks he is a bull. I go inside and he chases me like a bull. In his bull vision he cannot leave the enclosure because he cannot see the breaks in the wire fence, two overlapping half-circles of chain-link fence. I slip out, safe. A moment later he is able to see the way out and becomes a man as he escapes.

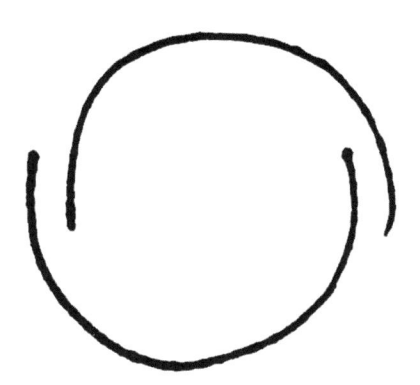

The Time of Turning

Sitting here
feeling deeply
in the silence
with myself for company

I know the last section
will be about
how difficult it is
how very difficult it has been
to grow up
with so many choices
and so little guidance.

The poignancy
of being human,
an ape with hands and imagination,
a child let loose
upon the face and body of the Mother Earth
with tremendous curiosity
developed into tremendous capacity
for both creation and destruction.
A child of wonder
born screaming/laughing into a whole-cloth universe
where drama and passion are warp and weft.
A universe with an affinity for surprise endings...

Who would have guessed?

The Human Race. The curse of Free Will.
Struggling
to be Born
in the Dark.
What does mature consciousness look like?
What is the Universe evolving
(through us)
this time?
What will it look like? Feel like?
Who will we be?

In our tenderness
We created parent-gods
to give a sense of safety
to the wilderness.
But the time has come
to leave the parental enclosures
and become parents ourselves to a brave new world.
Adults,
we shall commit adultery:
we shall become responsible
for our own happiness,
for the freedom of our wise and unwise choices,
for the happiness of our children's children's children
unto the seventh generation.
This is the Time of Turning.

References & Recommended Reading

Adair, Peter, Sacred Universe (2017)

Berry, Thomas; The Dream of the Earth

Berry, Thomas and Swimme, Brian, The Universe Story: From the Primordial Flaring Forth to the Ecozoic Era--A Celebration of the Unfolding of the Cosmos (1994)

Brown, Norman O., Life Against Death and Love's Body

Campbell, Joseph, The Way of the Animal Powers

Craighead, Meinrad, The Mother's Song

Davis, Elizabeth Gould, The First Sex (Penguin Books, Baltimore, 1971)

Davis, Wade, The Wayfinders

Eisenstein, Charles, The More Beautiful World Our Hearts Know is Possible (2013)

Ford, Clyde W., Compassionate Touch (Fireside/Parkside 1993)

Foster, Jeff, The Way of Rest: Finding the Courage to Hold Everything in Love (2016)

Glendinning, Chellis My Name is Chellis and I'm in Recovery from Western Civilization

Gould, Stephen J., Hen's Teeth and Horse's Toes: Further Reflections in Natural History (1983)

Hendrix, Harville, Getting the Love You Want (Harper & Row, 1988)

Katie, Byron, www.TheWork.com

Lechler, Walter, I Exist, I Need, I'm Entitled, (Doubleday & Company, Inc., Garden City, NY 1980)

Lourde, Audrey, excerpted from The Erotic as Power (1978)

Noble, Vicki, Motherpeace: A Way to the Goddess Through Myth, Art and Tarot

Shepherd, Philip, New Self,New World (2010) and Radical Wholeness (2017)

Silidker, Val, <u>Awaken to Wholeness Summit</u> (2017)

Sjoo, Monica & Mor, Barbara, <u>The Great Cosmic Mother</u> (1987)

Swimme, Brian, <u>The Universe is a Green Dragon</u>

Thompson, W.I. <u>The Time Falling Bodies Take to Light</u>

Tweedie, Irina, <u>Daughter of Fire</u> (Blue Dolphin, 1986)

Van der Kolk, Bessel, <u>The Body Keeps the Score</u> (2014)

Waters, Frank, <u>The Man Who Killed The Deer</u> (1941)

Grateful Acknowledgement

♥

To three dear friends without whose help and encouragement this second edition would not be in front of you now:

♥

Reverend Mary Francis Drake, who read the original and asked where her students could get this book! And for walking me through the somewhat daunting process of online self-publishing.

♥

Julia Eva Bacon, my graphic designer and dear friend, for her beautiful cover design using a photo of the Fragrant Apricot rose that grows in our sunroom. Julia patiently and lovingly helped me over many hurdles with illustrations.

♥

Tony Bacon, for the author photo and help with computer glitches and back-up. Tony is a whiz!

♥

And to my love, Peter Adair.

Gratitude for the title to Norman O. Brown whose book <u>Love's Body</u> slept at the head of my bed through two marriages.

About the Author

Caitlin Adair *lives in a clearing in the forest in Westminster West, Vermont, with her partner of over 30 years, Peter Adair. She lives close to the Earth. She particularly loves the miracle of flowers, fragrance, and the growing of food. She listens carefully to the flowing songs of Earth. She has been a dancer, mother, painter, gardener, poet, singer, world traveler and cleaner of houses. She is a grandma now. If you want to contact Caitlin, please email* Caitlin@sanctuaryvermont.com*.*

For more information: www.caitlinadair.com